北大社·普通高等院校"十二五"规划教材
21世纪职业教育规划教材·旅游系列

旅游英语（第二版）

袁智敏　主　编
余益辉　副主编
丁志明　参　编

内容简介

本书根据涉外导游工作对英语口语的需求编写，分为入境旅游和出境旅游两部分。

第1部分"入境旅游"（Inbound Tourism）由九个单元组成，内容涉及迎客和转移、登记入住、行程安排、市内观光、用餐、购买工艺品、参观茶园、参观丝绸博物馆和丝绸厂及处理投诉等方面。第2部分"出境旅游"（Outbound Tourism）由九个单元组成，内容涉及办理乘机手续、出入境、过海关、乘机、住酒店、货币兑换、用西餐、购物、参与游客自由活动及配合地陪工作等方面。每个单元包括本课导读、专业词汇、情景对话、必学句型、阅读材料和练习六个部分。为了方便读者查阅，书后附有练习答案、世界各国主要航空公司代码表、飞机型号表和总词汇表。

本书可作为旅游专业的教材，也可作为旅行社导游的工作手册。

图书在版编目（CIP）数据

旅游英语/袁智敏主编．—2版．—北京：北京大学出版社，2013.5
（全国高职高专规划教材·旅游系列）
ISBN 978-7-301-21508-1

Ⅰ．①旅… Ⅱ．①袁… Ⅲ．①旅游－英语－高等职业教育－教材 Ⅳ．①H31

中国版本图书馆 CIP 数据核字（2012）第 258921 号

书　　　　名：	旅游英语（第二版）
著作责任者：	袁智敏　主编
策划编辑：	李　玥
责任编辑：	李　玥
标准书号：	ISBN 978-7-301-21508-1/G·3526
出版发行：	北京大学出版社
地　　　址：	北京市海淀区成府路 205 号　100871
电　　　话：	邮购部 62752015　发行部 62750672　编辑部 62765126　出版部 62754962
网　　　址：	http://www.pup.cn　新浪官方微博：@北京大学出版社
电子信箱：	zyjy@pup.cn
印　刷　者：	北京圣夫亚美印刷有限公司
经　销　者：	新华书店

787 毫米×1092 毫米　16 开本　13.5 印张　329 千字
2005 年 8 月第 1 版
2013 年 5 月第 2 版　2021 年 8 月第 9 次印刷　总第 19 次印刷

定　　价：31.00 元（含光盘）

未经许可，不得以任何方式复制或抄袭本书之部分或全部内容。
版权所有，侵权必究
举报电话：010-62752024　电子信箱：fd@pup.pku.edu.cn

Preface I
第一版前言

中国旅游资源的魅力和旅游业的发展潜力强烈吸引了世界各国的旅游人士,中国旅游业正面临着持续发展的良机和挑战。要想使之获得飞速发展,就需要越来越多的专业人才加入到这个行业中来,这对我国的旅游教育事业,特别是培养高素质的旅游外语人才提出了更高的要求。

但纵观近年来培养的旅游专业学生和导游人员,能用地道的英语向海外游客介绍中国悠久的历史文化和秀丽的山水景色的,或独立带领国内游客畅游欧、美、澳洲的,为数不多。导游的外语水平成了制约我国旅游国际化发展的瓶颈。为此,笔者根据教学要求,集多年来的旅游英语口语教学经验,精心编写了《旅游英语》这本教材,以期能较快提高旅游专业学生的英语口语水平。

本书根据涉外导游工作对英语口语的需求编写,分为入境旅游和出境旅游两部分。

第1部分"入境旅游"(Inbound Tourism)由九个单元组成,旨在培养学生从事入境游导游工作、接待国外旅游者的能力,内容涉及迎客和转移、登记入住、行程安排、市内观光、用餐、购买工艺品、参观茶园、参观丝绸博物馆和丝绸厂及处理投诉等方面。第2部分"出境旅游"(Outbound Tourism)由九个单元组成,旨在培养学生从事出境游领队工作、带团出国观光旅游的能力,内容涉及办理乘机手续、出入境、过海关、乘机、住酒店、货币兑换、用西餐、购物、参与游客自由活动及配合地陪工作等方面。每个单元包括本课导读、专业词汇、情景对话、必学句型、阅读材料和练习六个部分。为了方便读者查阅,书后附有练习答案、世界各国主要航空公司代码表、飞机型号表和总词汇表。

本教材构思新颖,内容丰富,实用性强,比较全面地介绍了涉外导游工作的各个程序,不仅可作为旅游专业的教材,还可作为旅行社导游的工作手册。

本教材主编为袁智敏,副主编为余益辉,丁志明参编。在编写过程中,得到浙江旅游职业学院领导徐云松、汪亚民的支持和帮助,在此表示衷心感谢。

由于编者水平有限,编写时间仓促,疏漏和不足之处在所难免,恳请读者不吝指正。

编 者
2005年4月

Preface II
第二版前言

近年来，随着我国经济的快速发展和居民可支配收入的迅速提高，我国居民的出游人数及出游率也在快速增长。据世界旅游组织（UNWTO）预测，到2022年，中国将成为世界最大的旅游目的地市场和世界第四大客源输出国。作为国民经济新的增长点，中国旅游业在整个社会经济发展中的作用日益显现。旅游业的快速发展，需要越来越多的专业人才加入到这个行业中来，这对我国的旅游教育事业，特别是培养高素质的旅游外语人才提出了更高的要求。

但是纵观近年来培养的旅游专业学生和导游人员，能用地道的英语向海外游客介绍中国悠久的历史文化和秀丽的山水景色，或独立带领国内游客畅游欧、美、澳洲等旅游胜地的，为数不多。涉外导游人员的外语素质和交际水平，成了制约我国旅游业出入境市场发展的瓶颈。为此，笔者根据多年来从事旅游教育培训的经验以及精心收集的资料，编写了《旅游英语》一书，定于2005年出版，以期能较快提高旅游专业学生的口语水平，适应导游实际工作的需求。

近几年，旅游形势发生了很大的变化，因此，我们对本书进行了修订。本书第二版修正了部分词汇和句型，按照实际工作需要，修改或增加了部分章节的内容。本书构思新颖，内容丰富，实用性强，较全面的介绍了涉外导游接待服务工作的各个流程，不仅可作为旅游专业学生的导游英语教材，还可作为工作手册供旅行社涉外导游随查随用。

本书由袁智敏担任主编，余益辉担任副主编，丁志明为参编。在编写过程中，得到了浙江旅游局和浙江旅游职业学院有关领导的热情支持和帮助，在此表示衷心感谢。

由于编者水平有限，编写时间仓促，疏漏和不足之处在所难免，恳请读者不吝指正。

编　者

2012年4月

Contents
目　　录

Part I　INBOUND TOURISM　入境旅游 ··· 1
　Unit 1　Greeting and Transferring　迎客和转移 ································ 2
　Unit 2　Checking in at the Hotel　登记入住 ····································· 10
　Unit 3　Itinerary Planning　行程安排 ··· 18
　Unit 4　City Sightseeing　市内观光 ··· 25
　Unit 5　Dining at a Chinese Restaurant　用中餐 ······························· 33
　Unit 6　Visiting the Tea Garden　参观茶园 ····································· 41
　Unit 7　Shopping at the Arts and Crafts Stores　工艺品店购物 ············ 48
　Unit 8　Visiting the China Silk Museum and the Silk Factory　参观中国丝绸博物馆和丝绸厂 ··· 57
　Unit 9　Handling Complaints　处理投诉 ··· 64
Part II　OUTBOUND TOURISM　出境旅游 ······································ 71
　Unit 1　At the Airport（I）　在机场（1）
　　　　——Check-in at the Airport　办理登机手续 ··························· 72
　Unit 2　At the Airport（II）　在机场（2）
　　　　——Going through Immigration and Customs　办理出入境手续 ······ 83
　Unit 3　On the Airliner　在飞机上 ·· 95
　Unit 4　At the Hotel　在酒店 ··· 105
　Unit 5　Money Exchanging　货币兑换 ·· 117
　Unit 6　At Western Restaurants and Bars　在西餐厅和酒吧 ················ 124
　Unit 7　Shopping with Tourists　购物 ·· 132
　Unit 8　Free Activities　参与游客自由活动 ···································· 141
　Unit 9　Cooperating with the Local Guide　配合地陪工作 ·················· 148
Part III　Key to the exercises　练习答案 ··· 155
　Part I　Inbound Tourism　入境旅游 ·· 156
　Part II　Outbound Tourism　出境旅游 ··· 167
Part IV　Appendix　附录 ·· 177
Glossary　词汇表 ·· 181
References　参考文献 ·· 208

Part I

INBOUND TOURISM

入境旅游

Unit 1 Greeting and Transferring 迎客和转移

本课导读

迎客是整个旅游接待过程的第一步。英语里有 well begun is half done（良好的开端是成功的一半）的说法,可见开头的重要。一个好的导游员必须从一开始就要进入角色,做到热情周到,开朗幽默。其程序包括找到客人、问候客人、清点人数、确认行李、带客上车等。而转移与迎客是互不可分的一个整体,是迎客的必然延续。转移过程中,导游员要致欢迎词,作沿途讲解和对抵达城市、下榻饭店的介绍等。

Special Terms 专业词汇

baggage check	行李票	vacationing group	休假团
bring up the rear	殿后	study/survey group	考察团
CITS	中国国际旅行社	regular flight	定期航班
(China International Travel Service)		extra flight	加班机
international/domestic flight	国际/国内航班	charter	包机
local/national guide	地方/全程陪同	direct flight	直航班机
luggage/baggage	行李	passenger plane	客机
on behalf of...	代表……	baggage claim area	行李认领区
sit back	休息一下	peak/off season	旅游旺季/淡季
take the lead	前面带路	immigration control	入境检查
tidal bore	涌潮	emigration control	出境检查
tour leader	旅游团领队	formality	手续
travel service	旅行社	accommodation train	慢车
parking lot	停车场	arrival platform	下客站台
tour escort/leader	领队	behind schedule	晚点
information desk	问询处	berth/bunk	火车铺位
hand luggage	手提行李	caboose	乘务员车
checked luggage	托运行李	dining car	餐车
delayed flight	延误航班	dome car	旅游观赏车厢
terminal building	候机大厅	junket	公费旅游
locate	找出/定位	luxurious tour	豪华游
carrousel	（行李）传送带	make a sightseeing tour	游山玩水
government delegation	政府代表团		

Unit 1 Greeting and Transferring 迎客和转移

 Situational Conversations 情景对话

1. Greeting 迎接

Scene 1

(A: Local Guide; B: Tour Leader)

A: Excuse me, sir, but are you Mr. William Smith?

B: Yes, I am.

A: How do you do, Mr. William Smith! I'm Wang Feng, your local guide from CITS①.

B: How do you do, Mr. Wang! Nice to meet you.

A: Nice to meet you, too. Welcome to Hangzhou. Could you tell me whether everyone of the group is here, Mr. William Smith?

B: I'm sorry to say that one couple didn't come because of sudden illness. We have twenty three people including me now.

A: That's all right. But we've got to make some change in room arrangements.

B: Sorry to cause you so much trouble.

A: No trouble at all. Have all of the tourists got their luggage?

B: Let me see. Yes, they have.

A: Shall we bring them to the bus?

B: Sure. Take the lead please. I'll bring up the rear.

A: Ladies and gentlemen, attention, please. Now please follow me to the bus.

Scene 2

(A: Guide; B: Tour Leader; C: Stranger)

A: Excuse me, but are you Mr. Brown from Canada?

C: No. I'm Peter from America.

A: I'm so sorry.

C: Never mind②.

A: Excuse me. Are you Mr. Brown from Canada?

B: Yes, I am. Are you our local guide here?

A: Yes. My name is Li. Welcome to Hangzhou.

B: Thank you.

A: How was your trip?

B: Pretty good. People were chatting and drinking tea all the way. But this is an old group. They are getting off the train slowly now.

A: No hurry. But can I have the baggage check first?

B: Of course. Here you are. There are 18 pieces altogether.

A: Good. I'll see to it that they go to our hotel as soon as possible③. Is everybody here now?

B: Let me check. Yes, all here.

A: Before we move, could you tell the guests to follow my flag since it's so crowded here?

B: Sure. You go ahead and we will follow you.

Scene 3

(A: Guide; B: Tour Leader; C: Manager)

A: Excuse me, but aren't you Mr. Smith?

B: Yes, I am.

A: I'm a guide from the China Travel Service. My name is Peter Wang.

B: How do you do, Mr. Peter Wang!

A: How do you do? Our manager, Mr. Li has come to meet you. May I introduce him to you?

B: Of course.

A: This is our manager Mr. Li. This is Mr. Smith from the U.S.A.

C: Hello, Mr. Smith. Welcome to China.

B: Hello Mr. Li. It's really kind of you to come to meet me.

C: It's my pleasure. I hope you have enjoyed your trip.

B: Yes, very much. Thank you.

C: Hope you will have a good stay here, too.

B: I'm sure I will. Thanks a lot.

A: Your bag seems heavy. May I help you with it?

B: No, thanks. I can manage it by myself.

A: All right. Our car is waiting over there. Let's go.

2. Transferring 转移

Scene 1

(A: Guide; B: Tour Leader; C: Tour Member)

A: Good evening, ladies and gentlemen. Are we all on the bus?

B: Just a moment please. Mrs. Johnson is not here yet.

A: Where is she?

B: There she comes.

C: I'm sorry. Am I the last one?

A: Yes, but that's all right. I guess you are attracted by the beauty of the airport, aren't you?

C: Well, yes! But now I'm ready to go.

B: Yes.

A: OK. Ladies and gentlemen, on behalf of the China International Travel Service and our driver, I would like to extend our warmest welcome to you all. Welcome to Hangzhou! Welcome to the Paradise on Earth! Our Driver is Mr. Zhang who has a driving experience of 15 years, and my name is Li. During your stay in our city, Mr. Zhang and I will be at your disposal[④]. We'll do everything possible to make your visit a pleasant experience. If you have any problem or request, please do not hesitate to let us know.

Now, we are heading for our hotel, the Lake View Hotel, a luxurious four-star hotel located right on the famous West Lake. It takes about 40 minutes. So please sit back and relax yourselves while I'm giving you some general information of our city.

B: That's great.

A: Here is the largest river in our province, Qiantang River. It covers a distance of 610 kilometers and is known for its tidal bores.

B: Right. I've heard of it before and once saw it on TV. It was fascinating.

A: Now we have come to the lake side. Most part of the lake is lighted. When the lights are on, it's really attractive.

B: It must be! But we are also looking forward to seeing it in day time tomorrow.

A: Tomorrow comes very soon. And here is our hotel. Good night and have a good stay!

Scene 2

(A: Guide; B: Tourist)

A: Good evening, Madam and Sir. Welcome to Hangzhou.

B: Thank you. Thank you for your coming to meet us.

A: It's my pleasure. Now you've arrived at the paradise on earth.

B: Yes. We've heard of Hangzhou many times as the paradise on earth. What does "Hangzhou" actually mean?

A: This is a really good question. According to the geological research, the present city proper was part of the sea in the ancient times. If people wanted to come here, they could only come by boat. For that meaning in Chinese "Hang" is the word. And "Zhou" simply means an area.

B: Thank you very much. And what is Hangzhou famous for?

A: In general, Hangzhou is famous for its long history, beautiful scenery and abundant products. I'll give you more details while our trip goes on.

B: This is our first trip to your city. I was told it was a very popular scenic city among the Chinese.

A: They told you right. In China, there is an old saying which goes like this: Up in heaven there is paradise, down on Earth there are Suzhou and Hangzhou⑤. So, Chinese people consider Hangzhou as the paradise on Earth. Hangzhou saw its heyday during the Southern Song Dynasty, when it served as the capital for the whole China. Thus, Hangzhou is one of the six ancient capital cities in China.

B: How big is the city of Hangzhou?

A: The city covers an area of 16847 square kilometers with a population of 8.7 million. And it is still growing. As for the population in China, I have a piece of very important information for you, that is the No. 1.3 billion person in China was born in Beijing on January 6, 2005.

B: Look, there is a suspension bridge straight ahead of us.

A: Yes. The suspension bridge we are on is called Qiantang Bridge No. 3. Qiantang Bridge No. 1 is on your left hand side and No. 2 is on your right. We will build altogether 10 bridges across this river in the near future.

B: China is developing so fast. The whole country is like a huge construction site. No wonder people say the national bird of China is the crane.

A: You bet. Look at the skyscraper⑥ on your right. This is the second tallest building in Hangzhou——the Telecommunication Tower. It has 44 stories and is approximately 220 meters high.

B: I can see the city is growing fast.

A: Yes. It is growing taller and bigger. Now we are on a new road leading to the West Lake.

B: Oh, what a beautiful lake!

A: This is the famous West Lake in Hangzhou. Strange enough, there are altogether 36 west-lakes in China. But this one overshadows all the others.

B: How interesting! What are those plants in the lake?

A: They are lotus. The West Lake is famous for its lotus blossom in summer. Here we are at the Shangri-La Hotel. I'll ask the bellboy to take care of your luggage and I will help you to check in.

B: Thank you.

Notes 注释

① CITS 中国国际旅行社的英文缩写,全称为 China International Travel Service,是中国最大的涉外旅行社之一。

② never mind 没关系。

③ I'll see to it that they go to our hotel as soon as possible. 行李服务是涉外旅游团队服务的一个重要服务环节。导游员要确保客人的托运行李尽快送达所住饭店。

④ be at your disposal 任您使用,为您服务。

⑤ Up in heaven there is paradise, down on Earth there are Suzhou and Hangzhou. 上有天堂,下有苏杭。

⑥ skyscraper 摩天大楼。

Useful Sentences 必学句型

1. Excuse me, sir, but are you…
   对不起,请问先生您是不是……?

2. I'm Wang Feng, your local guide from…
   我叫王封,来自……,是你们的地陪。

3. Is this your first trip to Hangzhou?
   这是您第一次来杭州吗?

4. I'm sorry to say that…
   我很抱歉地说……

5. Sorry to cause you the trouble.
   给你带来麻烦,真不好意思。

6. I can manage it all right.
   我自己能行。

7. Ladies and gentlemen, may I have your attention, please?
   女士们，先生们，请大家注意一下好吗？
8. On behalf of the China International Travel Service and our driver, I would like to extend our warmest welcome to you all.
   我代表中国国际旅行社和我们的司机，向大家表示最热烈的欢迎。
9. I will be at your disposal.
   我将竭诚为您服务。
10. The city covers an area of…square kilometers with a population of…
    这个城市的面积为……，人口是……
11. I hope you have had a pleasant trip.
    我想你的旅途一定很愉快吧。
12. I hope you will have a good time in Hangzhou.
    希望你在杭州玩得愉快。

Passage Reading 阅读材料

Passage 1

Welcome Speech

Good evening, ladies and gentlemen. Welcome to Shanghai.

Please sit back and relax. Your luggage will be sent to the hotel by another bus, so you don't have to worry about it.

First, please allow me to introduce ourselves. Our driver is Mr. Zhang. He has 15 years of driving under his belt. So you are in very safe hands. My name is Mei Lifang, but you may just call me May. We are from Shanghai China International Travel Service. On behalf of Shanghai CIST, I'd like to extend a warm welcome to you all.

During your stay in our city, we'll do everything possible to make our visit a pleasant experience. If you have any problem or request, please don't hesitate to let us know. You are going to stay at the Peace Hotel, a time-honored and well located five-star hotel. As you'll stay in our city for two and a half days, you will do well to remember the number of our bus. The number is 72056. Let me repeat: 72056 is our bus number.

I hope you will enjoy your stay in my city.

Passage 2

Introduction to Hangzhou

Since ancient times, Hangzhou has been noted as a land flowing with milk and honey, if not an out-and-out Shangri-La. As the existing records hold it, a long, long time ago, this place was but a vast body of water connected with the present-day Pacific. An emperor journeyed here by boat for inspection. His boat was moored somewhere about today's children's palace of the city. Now to mark his trip the emperor named the place "Yuhang" which was later converted into Hangzhou, which literally means a place accessible only by boat.

The city rose to fame after the Grand Canal was completed in the Sui Dynasty some 1300 years ago. In the ensuing years, several kingdoms set up their capitals here. It was in the Southern Song Dynasty that Hangzhou saw its heyday. In 1275 the Italian traveler Marco Polo paid a visit to Hangzhou during his term of office as an envoy in the Yuan Dynasty. Under his pen, the city was depicted as "the most elegant and graceful city on earth".

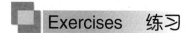

Exercises 练习

1. Reading and Translation

Good afternoon, ladies and gentlemen. Welcome to Shanghai. Please sit back and relax. Your luggage will be sent to the hotel by another bus. So you don't have to worry about it.

First, please allow me to introduce ourselves. Mr. Zhang is our driver. He has 20 years of driving under his belt, so you are in very safe hands. My name is Guo Qiang. We are from CITS Shanghai. On behalf of my company and my colleagues, I'd like to extend a warm welcome to you all.

During your stay in our city, Mr. Zhang and I will be at your disposal. We'll do everything possible to make your visit a pleasant experience. If you have any problem or question, please don't hesitate to let us know.

I hope you will have a good time in Shanghai.

2. Complete the Following Dialogues in English with the hints given in Chinese

(1) (A: Guide; B: Guest; C: Manager)

A: 对不起, 请问您是史密斯先生吗?

B: _____

A: 我是浙江中国国际旅行社的导游王永俊。

B: _____, Mr. Wang?

A: 你好。我们的林经理来接你了。我来介绍一下吧。这是我们的经理林先生, 这是来自美国太平洋旅游企业有限公司 (American Pacific Delight) 的史密斯先生。

C: 你好, 史密斯先生, 欢迎你来到杭州。

B: _____

C: Oh, it is a pleasure. 你的旅途一定很愉快吧。

B: _____

C: 这是你第一次来杭州吗, Mr. Smith?

B: _____

C: 希望你在杭州玩得愉快。

B: _____

A: 客人都在了, 我们上车吧。车子在停车场等我们呢。

(2) (A: Guide; B: Guest 1; C: Guest 2; D: Tour Leader)

A: Excuse me, but are you Mr. Brown from the United States of America?

B: 我不是, 我想你是弄错了。

A：_____

B：没关系。

C：哦，我是来自美国的旅游团成员。布朗先生是我们的领队，他在那儿。

A：Thank you.

A：对不起，你是来自美国的布朗先生吧？

D：_____

A：你好，布朗先生，欢迎来到杭州。我是中国青年旅行社的导游，叫刘伟。

D：_____

A：一路上好吗，布朗先生？

D：_____

A：人都到齐了吗？

D：_____

A：我们的车就在外面的停车场，我们走吧。

3. **Role-play**

Situation A

You are at the airport to meet a tour group of 25 people by the name of ZJCITS-050325. Its tour leader is Mr. Dow. Several groups have arrived. Find Mr. Dow, greet him and his group and show them to the bus according to the working procedure.

Situation B

You just met a couple who came from Shanghai to Hangzhou by train. You are on the way from the train station to Shangri-La Hotel where they are going to stay. Express your welcome to them and introduce to them what you see on the way.

Unit 2 Checking in at the Hotel 登记入住

本课导读

导游员在迎接客人之前需与客人将要下榻的饭店联系，确认客人的用房预订情况，包括用房数、用房类型等，以便客人抵达后能顺利入住。客人抵达酒店以后，导游应立即与酒店前台接洽，协助领队/客人办理入住手续。而酒店接待员则应礼貌地请客人出示护照、填写登记表、向客人分发钥匙等。导游在安排客人入住以后，要向客人简单介绍酒店的主要设施，如餐厅、酒吧、健身房等，同时要向客人说明第二天的大致行程和见面时间，之后方可向客人道别。

Special Terms 专业词汇

tour group	旅游团队	front office manager	前台部经理
book	预订	duty manager	值班经理
business center	商务中心	reception supervisor	接待部主管
card key	卡式钥匙	manager of room division	客房部经理
check in	入住	peep hole	猫眼
credit card	信用卡	revolving door	旋转门
double bed	双人床	receipt	收据
housekeeping	客房服务	bellboy/bellman	行李员
key slot	钥匙槽	health center	健身中心
king-size /queen-size bed	加大床/大床	bicycles for rent	自行车出租
lobby	大堂	breakfast voucher	早餐券
make a reservation	预订	registration form	登记表
passport	护照	luggage/meal delivery	送行李/餐
reception/front desk	前台/总台	registration form	登记表
receptionist	前台服务员	staircase	楼梯
information	问询处	elevator/lift	电梯
suite	套间	veranda	走廊/阳台
deluxe suite	豪华套间	beauty parlor/salon	美容部
presidential suite	总统套间	IDD telephone	国际直拨电话
single room	单人间	indoor swimming pool	室内游泳池
twin room	标准双人间	multifunction hall	多功能厅
assistant manager	大堂助理	room service	客房送餐服务

wardrobe	衣柜	lobby bar	大堂吧
wall lamp	壁灯		

Situational Conversations　情景对话

1. Group Check-in　团队入住

Scene 1

(A: Local Guide; B: Tour Leader; C: Receptionist)

C: Good evening! Welcome to our hotel.

A: Good evening! I'd like to have two suites, five singles and four twins.

C: Have you made a reservation?

A: Yes. We've booked them for our tour group from the Unite States. I'm from China International Travel Service and the group code is ZJCITS-A0509024 with 17 passengers.

C: I'm sorry, but I don't see your reservation here.

A: I'm sure we have made a reservation. I reconfirmed① it before I came. Could you check again or contact the Sales Department?

C: All right. Let me check again. Ah, yes, here it is. Two suites, five singles and four twins for CITS.

B: Any problem?

A: No, everything is all right.

B: Are the rooms ready?

C: Yes, they are. But can I have your passports, please?

B: Sure. Here you are.

C: Thank you. Would you please fill in these registration forms?

B: The forms are finished. Shall we have the keys to our rooms?

C: Here are the keys. Have a good stay in our hotel.

B: Thank you. We will.

Scene 2

(A: Guide; B: Tour Leader; C: Receptionist)

A: Mr. Smith, let's first make sure of the rooming. We've booked 11 twins for 22 people according to the name list you sent us. Is that OK?

B: Well, thank you. But one of the tour members, that's number 8 on the name list, insists on having a single room. Is it possible to split one twin room into two singles?

A: I see. Let me talk with the receptionist about it. (To the receptionist) Hello, I'm the local guide of the Inter Pacific Tour.

C: Just a moment, sir. Let me check the list. Yes, we are holding 11 twins for two nights for you.

A: That's right. But there is a change. Can we have 10 twins and 2 singles instead?

C: Yes, we do have single rooms at the moment. But you'll have to pay for the other single.

A: I see. What's the room rate?

C: The rate is RMB2 000 per night. You will stay for two nights.

B: O. K. Here is RMB4 000.

C: Thank you. May I see your group visa, please?

B: Yes, sure. Here you are.

C: Thank you. Here are the registration forms. Please help your clients fill them out. And here are the keys. I hope you will enjoy your stay at our hotel.

B: Thank you. We will.

2. Walk-in Check-in 无预订散客入住

(A: Guide; B: Receptionist; C: Tourist)

A: Excuse me. I'm from CYTS (China Youth Travel Service) Zhejiang. My guests Allan and his wife have just arrived with their two children.

B: Welcome to our hotel. Have you made a reservation?

A: No. Could I have two adjacent rooms② with twin beds?

B: Let me see…sorry, we don't have any adjacent rooms left. Would you like to have two double rooms? One of them faces the beautiful West Lake.

A: Allan, what's your idea?

C: Can I have two double rooms facing the lake?

B: No, I'm sorry. It's high season③. Lots of tourists are flooding into our city, so it's difficult to get rooms facing the lake in our hotel without reservations.

C: OK, I'll take the two rooms you've offered.

B: Would you please fill in④ this registration form?

C: Certainly. By the way, I'd like to confirm the room charge.

B: Yes. The rate is RMB2 500 for each.

C: What is the check-out time?

A: The check-out time is 12:00 noon.

C: And what are the service hours for the coffee shop? We'd like to get a bit to eat.

B: Its opens from 9:00 a. m. to 12:00 p. m.. Here are your room keys. Have a nice stay.

3. FIT Check-in 有预订散客入住

Scene 1

(A: Receptionist; B: Guide; C: Tourist)

A: Good evening. What can I do for you, sir?

B: I'm a guide from Zhejiang OTC (Overseas Tourist Company). We've booked a twin-bed room with bath three weeks ago for Mr. John Grimes.

A: Just a moment, please. Mr. Grimes. I'll check the arrival list. Yes, we do have a reservation for him. Would you please ask him to fill out this form when I prepare the key card for him?

B: Sure. Can I use your pen for a minute, please?

A: Here you are.

B: Mr. Grimes, would you please fill in this form?

C: Yes, of course. But what shall I put under room number?

A: Leave it there. I'll put it in for you later on.

C: Here you are. I hope I have filled everything correctly.

A: Let me see. Yes, everything is correct. Here is your key, Mr. Grimes. Your room number is 1818. On the 18th floor. And you can sign for your meals and drinks in the restaurants and the bars in the hotel[5] by showing your key. So please make sure you always have it with you.

C: OK. I'll take care of it.

B: All right Mr. Grimes, now let me get a bellboy and ask him to take you to your room.

C: Yes, thank you very much.

B: Enjoy your stay here, Mr. Grimes. See you tomorrow.

C: Thanks. See you tomorrow.

Scene 2

(A: Receptionist; B: Guide; C: Tourist)

B: Good afternoon. I would like to have a room for my friend.

A: Good afternoon, sir. Single or double?

B: Single, please.

A: Have you made a reservation?

B: Yes. He sent your hotel an e-mail last week from Beijing, but he didn't receive a confirmation letter.

A: May I know his name, please?

B: His name is Taylor.

A: Yes, we've received an e-mail from Mr. Taylor. And we are holding a room for him.

B: That's great. How much for a day?

A: It's RMB1 200 per night.

B: Mr. Taylor, the room rate is RMB1 200 per night, how do you like it?

C: All right. I'll take it.

A: How long do you plan to stay, Mr. Taylor?

C: Until Wednesday. I'll check out on Wednesday morning.

A: Would you please fill in the registration form, Mr. Taylor? I'll get a bellboy to take your bags and show you to your room.

B: Thank you very much.

A: Are you here on business, Mr. Taylor?

B: It's partly for business and partly for pleasure[6]. This is my first trip to Shanghai and I'm very eager to visit the city. So I may spend the first day or two just sightseeing.

A: Very good. This is your room key. It's room 818. Enjoy yourself.

B: Thanks a lot.

Notes 注释

① reconfirm 再确认，这是旅游行业里一个重要的步骤。所有的预订在团队即将抵达时都必须进行再确认，以确保团队接待的顺利操作。
② adjacent rooms 相邻的房间
③ high season 旺季，淡季为 low season。
④ 入住酒店必须填写住宿登记表。"填"既可用 fill in，也可用 fill out，但两者有所区别。fill in 表示"填写"，而 fill out 则表示"填好"。
⑤ 在餐厅或酒吧你可以签单。也就是说可以不用当时付现金而等到离店时一起结账。
⑥ for business 出差，for pleasure 游玩。一半出差，一半游玩。

Useful Sentences 必学句型

1. What can I do for you, sir?
   需要帮忙吗，先生？
2. Have you made a reservation?
   你有预订吗？
3. Do you want a single room or a double room?
   你是想要单人间还是双人间？
4. How many people are there in your party?
   你们一起有几个人？
5. Could you fill in this registration form?
   请你填一下这个住宿登记表。
6. You may keep your key until you check out.
   离店之前你可以自己拿着（房间）钥匙。
7. What are the service hours for the coffee shop?
   咖啡厅从几点开到几点？
8. How long do you plan to stay?
   你准备住几天？
9. May I help you with your bags, sir?
   需要我帮你拿行李吗，先生？
10. In whose name has the reservation been made?
    你是用谁的名字预订的？
11. May I confirm your departure date?
    我可以核对一下你的离店时间吗？
12. I would like to extend my stay by two days.
    我想续住两天。
13. We will inform you when the room is available.
    房间好了我们会告诉你的。

14. How many pieces of luggage do you have in all?
    你们总共有几件行李?
15. How do you spell your name, sir?
    你的名字怎么写,先生?

Passage Reading　阅读材料

Passage 1

Ladies and gentlemen, may I have your attention, please? I'd like to tell you something about the hotel we're going to stay in. This hotel is a first-rate hotel and has been chosen as the favorite place to stay by VIPs, official guests and businessmen from all over the world. There are over 350 rooms of international standard, including single rooms, double rooms and suites. There are two spacious Chinese restaurants offering all styles of Chinese cooking. They are located on the seventh floor. On the first floor, there is a deluxe western-style restaurant. Tomorrow morning we are going to have our breakfast there. There are also a bar, a 24-hour café and an outdoor patio with drinks. If you want to do some exercises, you can go to the health center, where there are billiard room, bowling alley and indoor swimming poor. They are ready to serve you at your convenience. If you want to have more details, you can get a brochure from the Front Desk. If you have any questions, please feel free to ask me. Thank you for your attention.

Passage 2

Good evening, ladies and gentlemen. Welcome to the Central Hotel. Your room keys and breakfast vouchers are in the envelopes on this table. They are arranged in alphabetical order. Please take the one which bears your name. Breakfast is served from 7:00 a.m. to 10:00 a.m. at the restaurant on the seventh floor. Upon your arrival there tomorrow morning, please hand the waiter your voucher. We will leave the hotel at 9:00 for sightseeing tomorrow. So we've arranged your wake-up call for 7:00. Those who want to get up earlier can contact with the operator to set yours for whatever time you like. We will stay here for two nights. So you don't need to pack tomorrow morning. The door of your room locks automatically. Please make sure that you have your room key with when you leave the room. The tap water in your room is not drinkable. Please drink mineral water or the water in the flask. Your baggage will be delivered to your room soon. Good night ladies and gentlemen and see you tomorrow at 9:00.

Exercises　练习

1. **Reading and Translation**

   The Museum of the First Qin Emperor's Terracotta Army

   In March 1974 when several farmers were sinking a well about 1.5 kilometers east of the First Qin Emperor's Mausoleum, they came upon many fragments of terracotta figures, the results of archaeological excavation showed that it was an oblong pit with terracotta warriors and horses. In

1976, two more pits were discovered 20 meters and 25 meters north of the former one respectively. They were then named Pit 1, Pit 2, and Pit 3 by order of discovery. The three pits cover a total area of 22 780 square meters.

The new discovery stirred up a sensation all over the world. In order to provide the historic artifacts with adequate protection, a museum was set up upon the approval of the State Council in 1975 and was officially open to the public on October 1, 1979. As one of the top ten places of historic interest in China, the Museum of the First Qin Emperor's Terracotta Army was listed as the world heritage by UNSECO in 1987.

2. Complete the Following Dialogues in English with the hints given in Chinese

(1) (A: Receptionist; B: Guide; C: Guest)

A: Good evening. _____, sir?

B: 两星期前我的客人 Tom Jordan 预订了一个大床间和一个标准间。

A: _____ his last name, please?

B: J-O-R-D-A-N, Jordan.

A: 谢谢。请您稍候，我查一下抵达统计表……是的，我们有他的预订，是一个大床间和一个标准间。大床间是给 Mr. 和 Mrs. Jordan 的，标准间是给 Betty 和 Mary 的，对吗？

B: _____

A: 请你让他填一下这张住宿登记表好吗？

B: _____

A: 我可以再确认一下他的离店时间吗？

B: _____ on the 9th.

A: Mr. Jordan，你是用什么付账的？

C: _____

A: 能不能把你的信用卡给我刷一下？

C: _____

A: 谢谢。

(2) (A: Receptionist; B: Guide; C: Guest)

B: Good afternoon. I would like to have a room.

A: 下午好，先生。你是要单人间还是双人间？

B: Single, please.

A: 请问你有预订吗？

B: Yes. I sent you a reservation by E-mail from Beijing last week, but I haven't got a reply.

A: _____?

B: The name is Taylor.

A: 是的，我们收到你的邮件了。我们给泰勒先生留了一个房间。

B: That's great. _____?

A: 每晚 1 200 元。

B: Mr. Taylor, the room rate is RMB1 200. _____?

C: That's right. I'll take it.

A: Mr. Taylor, 你准备住几天?
C: Until Wednesday. I'll _____ on Wednesday morning.
A: Would you please _____ the registration from, Mr. Taylor? Then I'll take your bags and _____ to your room.
C: Thank you very much.

3. Role-play

Situation A

You are working as a receptionist. Now a couple of American just came into your hotel and coming to the front desk. Greet them and check them in properly.

Situation B

The tour leader of a group of 30 British has just finished the check-in and is ready to deal with the delivery of the suitcases. You are a bellboy on duty. Work with the tour leader and do your job in a good manner.

Unit 3　Itinerary Planning 行程安排

本课导读

在旅游团抵达之前，地陪通常应该仔细阅读接团计划，了解客人的情况以及他们的要求，并据此制定出初步的行程安排。当然，一个旅游团的行程的最终决定是要跟领队或全陪商量进行的。因此，在团队入住以后，地陪应及时和领队或全陪商量次日的行程安排。在行程安排的过程中，地陪应认真听取领队或全陪的意见。在发生意见不一致的情况下，要在平等的基础上，本着客人利益至上的原则进行处理，切忌将自己的主观意见强加给别人。

Special Terms 专业词汇

Itinerary	行程；活动安排	sycamore tree	法国梧桐
be settled	安排好了	sweet osmanthus	桂花树
relaxing	休闲的，从容的	camphor	樟树
lake cruise	游湖	lotus	荷花
take the boat	坐船	plum	梅花
dock	船码头	chrysanthemum	菊花
tourist attraction	旅游点	tulips	郁金香
travel	旅游/旅行	cedar	雪松
tourism	旅游业	departure	出发
tourist assets	旅游资源	excursion	远足；游览
tourist boom	旅游热	tentative	暂定的
tourist ghetto	度假村	memorial hall	纪念馆
tourist resort	旅游胜地	flexibility	灵活性
theme park	主题游乐公园	city tour	城市游
theater restaurant	演剧餐厅	package tour/trip	包价旅游
monastery/temple	寺庙	sightseeing trip	观光旅游
lagoon	泻湖	conducted/guided tour	有导游的旅游
silt	淤泥	family group	家庭旅行团
causeway	堤	special-interest tour	特殊兴趣游
circumference	周长	optional tour	选择性旅游
dredge up	挖掘，疏浚	at your request	按照您的要求
weeping willows	柳树	private residential garden	私家园林

imperial garden	皇家园林	set out/start off	出发
monastic garden	寺庙园林	have a break	休息
scenic spot	风景点	historical relics	历史遗迹

Situational Conversations 情景对话

1. Planning a Boat Cruise on the West Lake 安排坐船游西湖

(A: Local Guide; B: Tour Leader)

B: It seems everything else is settled. Shall we have a discussion on the itinerary, Mr. Wang?

A: Oh, yes. Have you got anything special in mind that you would like to see?

B: I think you know your city better than I do. But this is an old group. Everything has to be slow and relaxing.

A: I see. So in the morning, we will leave the hotel at 9:00 for the cruise on the West Lake.

B: At what time does the boat leave?

A: Ten thirty.

B: Why do we leave so much earlier?

A: We will visit a park before we take the boat.

B: I see. But do we have to do that?

A: No. We can drive pretty close to the dock.

B: Can we do that and leave the hotel later?

A: No problem if you like. We can put our departure off① to a quarter to ten in that case.

B: That sounds perfect.

2. Planning the Itinerary of Hangzhou 安排杭州游行程

(A: Local Guide; B: Tourist)

A: Mr. Allen, now that you've finished with your check-in, before you rest, shall we have a brief discussion on what we are going to do tomorrow?

B: Yes. You are very considerate. When shall we start tomorrow morning?

A: I planned to leave at 9:00. Is that all right?

B: Yes, that will be fine. Will we have a busy day tomorrow?

A: Not really. We will have a boat ride on the West Lake in the morning after visiting a beautiful park. Lunch will be in a restaurant near the attractions.

B: That sounds very pleasant. I'm looking forward to it.

A: For the afternoon, we will tour a Buddhist temple called Lingyin Temple. And then we will have an excursion② to a tea farm where you will learn about the green tea.

B: The green tea arouses my interest. But we have seen quite a few Buddhist temples.

A: You are right. But I can promise you something very different in this temple. There are a hill of stone carvings and grottos aged from 700 to over 1000 years. They are worth visiting.

B: OK. We will do that then. Thank you for your telling me this.

A: It's my pleasure.

3. Discussing a Visit to Chairman Mao Memorial Hall 讨论参观毛主席纪念堂

(A: Guide; B: Tour Leader)

B: Miss Li, shall we start discussing the itinerary?

A: Yes, if you are ready. I've worked out a tentative itinerary③ here. Please go over it and let me hear your opinion on it.

B: You are efficient. Let me see. Don't you think it would be better to visit Chairman Mao Memorial Hall on Sunday rather than on a weekday.

A: Why is that? It is very crowded on Sundays.

B: That's exactly what I mean. We'd like to see how the Chinese people pay homage to④ this great man.

A: If we go on Sunday, we will spend several hours waiting in the line. We will have to cancel the other destination we have planned.

B: I don't see what the problem would be with seeing Chairman Mao Memorial Hall and the other places we talk about all on the same day.

A: I don't think you realize how many people will be visiting there on Sunday, and how long it will take us to go through these sites.

B: We would really like to see it on Sunday. Why don't we visit a few more places of interest before lunch.

A: Whatever you prefer.

B: We can arrange our lunch in a fast-food restaurant instead of this fancy Dragon Restaurant.

A: That will save our situation.

B: Thank you for your flexibility.

A: You are welcome.

4. Discussing the Itinerary for Beijing Tour   讨论北京游行程

(A: Guide; B: Tourist)

A: This is the tentative plan I've made for the following days. Please go it over. Are there any special places you are interested in?

B: I have an itinerary provided by the travel agency in the U.S. They have listed the places we are supposed to see here.

A: May I see the list, please?

B: Here you are. But I'm sure you know much better than those in the far U.S. You are the boss now. We will listen to you.

A: Thank you for your trusting me. According to my plan, the first day, that's tomorrow, to start the day, we will visit the largest square in the world, Tian'anmen Square. Then I'll show you to the Palace Museum right to the north of the square. Before lunch, we will have a tour to the Summer Palace where our lunch is reserved.

B: That sounds very attractive.

A: The morning is a bit tight⑤ but the afternoon will be relaxing. We will go to see the pandas in the zoo before visiting a souvenir shop.

B: Yes. We would like to buy some souvenir very much.

A: The second day will be long. We will go out of the city to the Ming Tombs and the Great Wall.

B: That would be tough. Do I have to climb the Great Wall?

A: It's all up to you. We'll see on the spot⑥.

B: What will we do on the third day?

A: We'll take you to a big and famous temple, the Temple of Heaven. After lunch, we'll have to leave for the airport.

B: Everything sounds great. Thank you very much.

A: You're welcome. See you tomorrow at 9:00 then.

5. Discussing the Itinerary for the Tour of China 讨论中国游行程

(A: Tour Leader; B: Guide)

A: How is the itinerary you've prepared for our group? Did you receive the fax that we sent to your company?

B: Yes, I did. Here is a copy of the itinerary I've prepared for your group. Please read it to see if there is a need of any change.

A: We're visiting a hutong in Beijing. That's marvelous. I'm sure everyone on the group will be excited to learn about the visit.

B: A visit to Children's Palace has been arranged in Shanghai. There you can see children learning all kinds of skills such as singing, dancing, drawing, writing calligraphy, learning English and so on.

A: That will be fun. And Mrs. Johansson and several other ladies, in particular, will appreciate the opportunity because they used to work at kindergartens.

B: The Church visiting is put in Hangzhou, where the itinerary is more relaxing.

A: Where are we going to have the bicycle riding?

B: I planned it in Lijiang, Yunnan Province. The landscape there is worth seeing in that way.

A: It's very considerate of you. I'm glad to have you be my national guide. I can almost see a happy and successful cooperation now.

B: Thank you. I'm sure we will have it.

Notes 注释

① 推迟出发时间。
② excursion 一般用于去离市区稍远的地方的团体旅游。
③ to work out a tentative itinerary 制定出一个暂定的行程。
④ pay homage to somebody 向某人表示敬意。
⑤ tight 指行程紧，也可用于资源等的紧张，如 The hotel rooms in Shanghai are always tight.
⑥ on the spot 现场/当场，如 pay on the spot 指现付。

Useful Sentences 必学句型

1. Shall we have a discussion on the itinerary?
   我们来讨论一下行程吧。

2. Have you got anything special in mind that you would like to see?
   你有没有特别想要去看的地方？

3. This is the tentative plan I've worked out. Would you please go over the details?
   这是我列的一个暂时的行程，请你过目看一下。

4. Perhaps you would like visit the old part of Hangzhou?
   或许你想去看看杭州的老城区？

5. It might be a good idea to…
   也许去……是个好主意。

6. For the afternoon, we will tour to…
   下午我们要去参观……

7. It's all up to you.
   你看着决定吧。

8. Please read/check it to see if there is a need of any change.
   请看/检查一下看看是否需要有什么更改。

9. We have a number of places that are worth visiting.
   我们有好多值得参观的地方。

10. I think we'd better make it 10:30, in case we get caught in the traffic.
    我看我们最好还是定在10:30，以防万一碰到堵车。

11. Wouldn't it be better to…?
    ……会不会更好一点？

12. I think you will find…interesting.
    我想你会对……感兴趣的。

 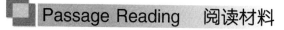

Passage Reading 阅读材料

Seal-cutting

Seal-cutting is a unique part of the Chinese cultural heritage. It is traditionally listed along with painting, calligraphy and poetry as one of the "four arts" which an accomplished scholar is supposed to master. The art dated back about 3700 years to the Yin Dynasty and originated from the cutting of oracle inscriptions on tortoise shells. It flourished in the Qin Dynasty, when people engraved their names on utensils and documents to show ownership. Lots of this grew the cutting of personal names on small blocks of horn, jade, or wood, namely, the seals as we know today.

Character on seals may be cut in relief or in intaglio (凹雕). The materials for seals could be wood, stone, horn, red-stained Changhua stone, jade, agate, crystal, ivory, or even gold.

Seals cut as works of art should be remarkable in three aspects——calligraphy, composition and the engraver's handwork. The artist should be good at writing various styles of the Chinese script. He should know how to arrange within a small space a number of characters——some with many strokes and others with very few——to achieve a graceful effect. He should also be familiar with the various materials——stone, brass or ivory——so that he may apply the cutting knife with the right exertion, technique, and even rhythm.

Exercises 练习

1. Reading and Translation

At 9 o'clock we left the hotel. We also had constant rain this day. However, the whole group had a very high spirit for the sightseeing: Dr. Sun Yatsen Memorial Hall, Cheng Family Temple, and Nanyue Museum in the morning and Shamian Island in the afternoon.

As it was the last day of the trip many guests wanted to do shopping. Miss Wu led us to the Friendship Store on Huanshi East Road which is a good place for Chinese silks, garments, jewelry, arts and crafts, curios, Foshan paper cut, porcelain and lacquer ware. The guests were so interested in the items in the Store that we had to put off our dinner which had been arranged beforehand at 5:30 till 7:30. At dinner Mrs. Pike commented that Guangzhou maintained its unique culture traditions different from the other cities in China, including its distinctive delicious, world-famous cuisine which all the guests liked so much.

2. Complete the Following Dialogues in English with the hints given in Chinese

(1) (A: Guide; B: Tour Leader)

B: 王先生，其他事情都安排好了，我们来讨论一下我们的行程吧。

A: Oh, yes. Have you got anything special in mind that you would like to see?

B: 你比我更了解你的城市。但是我们这是个老人团，所以一切都得慢慢来，放轻松点。

A: I see. So in the morning, we will leave the hotel at 9:00 am for the cruise on the West Lake.

B: _____

A: 10:30。

B: _____

A: 坐船之前我们还要参观一个公园。

B: I see. But do we have to do that?

A: No, _____

B: Can we do that and 晚一些离开饭店？

A: No problem if you like. 这样的话我们可以推迟到九点四十五分出发。

B: 这样很好。

(2) (A: Travel Clerk; B: Guest)

A: Good morning!

B: _____

A: 需要帮忙吗？

B: My wife and I want to see the places of interest in Hangzhou. 你能给我们安排一下吗？

A: _____

B: 两天，明天和后天。

A: The first day, 你可以参观北线，第二天去看南线。

B: _____

A: The north routine includes _____, the south routine covers _____

B: 听起来不错，这要多少钱？

A: 每人700元。

B: _____

A: 除了上述所有景点的门票，It also includes a private car and guide for two days and two lunches.

B: The price sounds reasonable. We will take it. 我们需要现在就付钱还是……

A: _____, 或行程完了以后也可以。

B: Thank you. 能不能让导游明天早上九点到望湖宾馆来接我们？

A: _____, 请把您的房间号码留给我们好吗？

B: Sure. It's 218.

A: 导游明天肯定会来接你们的。再见！

B: 谢谢，再见。

3. Role-play

Situation A

Mr. Smith, a foreign teacher working in Hangzhou, intends to have a one-day tour in Hangzhou. Help him work out an itinerary. Try to cover most of the well-known places in an efficient way.

Situation B

Philip and his wife come to you for an arrangement of a four-day tour including Hangzhou, Shanghai and Suzhou. Plan the tour for them.

Unit 4 City Sightseeing 市内观光

本课导读

观光游览是旅游的主要目的。在旅游的各个要素中，观光游览所占的比重是最大的。因此，在导游过程中，导游员在做好其他服务的基础上，对游客的观光游览应投入更多的精力。导游员要充分掌握景区及其相关的知识并随着景区情况的变化进行及时的补充。在讲解过程中不能千篇一律，要做到因人而异。对不同年龄、不同职业、不同层次、不同文化背景和不同兴趣的客人要做到详略得当、繁简适宜、深浅适度，同时还要将知识性和趣味性结合起来。

Special Terms 专业词汇

entrance/way in	入口	sand stone	砂岩
exit/way out	出口	crustal movement	地壳运动
gate	大门	sutras pillar	经幢
ticket	门票	Goddess of Mercy	观音
admission/entrance fee	门票费	Zen sect	禅宗
gate	大门	four heavenly protectors	四大天王
temple complex	寺院	become enlightened	成佛
grotto	石窟	statue	雕像
hand posture/gesture	手印	ancient pagoda	古塔
Bodhisattva	菩萨	pavilion	亭子
Sakyamuni	释迦牟尼	tower	楼/阁
Maitreya Buddha	弥勒佛	terrace	露台
Skanda / Veda	韦驮	up-turning eaves	翘檐
plaque	匾额	stele/stone tablet	石碑
clay	黏土	stupa	覆钵式塔
central axis	中轴线	threshold	门槛
architecture	建筑	arch bridge	拱桥
historical relics	历史古迹	stalactite	石钟乳
the holy relics of the Buddha	舍利子	stalagmite	石笋
peak flying from afar	飞来峰	reclining Buddha	卧佛
the crazy monk	济公	rockery	假山
lime stone	石灰岩	persecute	迫害

exonerate	平反	restore	恢复原貌
destroy	毁坏	give me back my territory	还我河山
renovate	重修	mural	壁画

 Situational Conversations　情景对话

1. A Visit to Lingyin Temple　参观灵隐寺

Scene 1

(A: Local Guide; B: Tour Leader)

A: Here we are at the entrance of the Lingyin Temple.

B: It is such a huge place. Why is it called Lingyin Temple?

A: The founder of the temple was an Indian monk. He wanted to live here as a hermit, because he believed that this was a place for souls①. So he named this temple Lingyin, which means Soul's Retreat Temple.

B: How old did you say the temple was?

A: It was first built in 326AD. So it is over 1600 years old. Though it has been destroyed and rebuilt many times.

B: What happened to the temple during the Cultural Revolution?

A: That is a good question. As a matter of fact, Lingyin Temple is the only temple which survived the Cultural Revolution here in Hangzhou. And we owe this to our late Premier Zhou Enlai. He ordered a high wall to be put up around the temple, and no one was allowed to enter the complex.

B: What about the monks, then?

A: They were sent home at that time.

Scene 2

(A: Tourist; B: Guide)

A: Woo, look, what big guys they've got here.

B: This is the Heavenly King's Hall②. Here you can see four guardians, two on each side. They work together to keep the world in peace, prosperity and harmony.

A: Liu, I have a question for you. Why do two of them look kind and the other two are mean and ferocious?

B: Chinese people believe to win peace you have to use both soft and tough tactics. Or, you may call it the balance of "Yin" and "Yang" in Chinese conception. Here in the shrine, facing the main entrance, sits Maitreya Buddha③, or more popularly known as Laughing Buddha. He is the symbol of happiness in China, as Chinese people say "a carefree mind, a fatty kind"④.

A: Oh, we do have a couple of Laughing Buddha in our group!

B: Here we can see the first treasure in this temple, the statue of Veda⑤. It is the oldest one here, more than 800 years old. And monks say the whole statue was carved out of one piece of huge camphor tree trunk. It is a nice piece, isn't it?

A: Absolutely.

B: Now let's go on to the Grand Hall. You can take photos here, with the Grand Hall as the background.

A: Look at the big trees. They must have been here for hundreds of years.

B: Yes. They are camphor trees. They live very long. Now we've come to the statue of the Buddha.

A: Oh, the Buddha here is so impressive!

B: This is the biggest sitting wooden Buddha in China, another treasure in this temple.

A: Was it made out of one piece of wood again?

B: Of course not. It was made up of 24 pieces of camphor wood. In early 1949, the front part of this hall collapsed, and it destroyed three smaller Buddha here. It was restored in the year 1956 under the instruction of Zhou Enlai. This statue is 19.6 meters high, to match the height of the hall.

A: How high is the building?

B: 33.6m or 110 feet. And the statue was coated with 3 kilos, or 104 ounces of pure gold. His gesture shows that he is giving lectures to his disciples.

A: Why is his hair blue?

B: Blue is the color of the sky, so he is considered as high as the sky.

A: I see.

2. Visiting Jade Buddha Temple 参观玉佛寺

(A: Local Guide; B: Tourist)

A: Mr. Richard, how do you do?

B: How do you do, Mr. Zhang?

A: How lucky you have such a fine day today to tour the Jade Buddha Temple. Are you ready to start?

B: Yes. We'll put ourselves in your hand from now on.

A: Thanks. It takes about half an hour to get there.

B: All right. We eagerly want to know the history of the temple. Could you give us some information about it?

A: Yes, with pleasure. The Jade Buddha Temple was built in 1882. It is one of the famous Buddhist temples south of the Changjiang River. Enshrined there are two white jade statues of Sakyamuni brought from Burma, one in a sitting posture and the other in a reclining posture.

B: Thank you for your explanation.

A: It's my pleasure. Now, let's go inside to have a look.

B: All right. Let's go.

A: This is the main hall of the temple.

B: The construction of this hall is so outstanding. It's not only extremely high, but quite magnificent as well.

A: Quite so. In Chinese, we call it "Da Xiong Bao Dian", meaning the Grand Hall. From the ground up to the roof it is briefly thirty feet high.

B: It's wonderful!

A: This is the precious jade statue of Sakyamuni brought from Burma more than one hundred years ago.

B: It was carved out of pure jade, wasn't it?

A: Yes, certainly. It's made of pure jade, indeed.

B: It must be a very precious and priceless treasure. I've been to many countries, yet I haven't seen such an honorable thing.

3. Cruise on Huangpu River 游黄浦江

(A: Guide; B: Tourist)

A: Now, Miss Jenny, we've started our cruise on the Huangpu River. The whole trip takes about three hours.

B: We're very interested in sailing along the river, as we can enjoy the beautiful scenery on both sides. Could you be kind enough to tell us something about the River?

A: Certainly. This river rises in Jiaxing County, Zhejiang Province. It runs through the city proper of Shanghai to meet the Changjiang River at Wusong, totaling 80 kilometers long with an average width of 400 meters. A boat trip to the Changjiang River enables one to be intoxicated with the magnificent view on both sides of the Huangpu River.

B: Ah, it's marvelous!

A: Now, we can take a full view of the Bund. This is Shanghai Mansion and that is the Bank of China.

B: Shanghai is really a marvelous harbor! There are so many ships!

A: Yes. Some of them are from foreign countries. That big one comes from the U.S.A.

B: True. Nowadays, the trade between US and China is increasing rapidly.

A: There's an acrobatics show downstairs right now. Would you like to see it?

B: That's a good idea. Let's go.

4. A Tour to the Palace Museum 参观故宫

(A: Guide; B: Tourist)

A: Good morning, Mr. Taylor. According to our schedule, today we're going to visit the Palace Museum. Are you ready now?

B: Good morning, Mr. Chen. I'm anxious to have a sightseeing there. But it looks like to rain. I want to get my raincoat. Just a moment, please. I'll be right back.

A: Take your time. I'll be waiting for you here.

B: Everything is OK now. Let's set off.

A: Now, we are standing on the grounds of the imperial palace.

B: Oh! It is gorgeous and elaborate, indeed.

A: This is the world-famous Forbidden City where once emperors, empresses and their families lived.

B: Yes. I can feel the grandness.

A: Let's move on.

B: What exquisite carvings! Mr. Chen, what's that white terrace?

A: That's the marble terrace on which the three main halls of the front part of the palace were built.

B: I'm eager to see what they look like.

A: Mr. Taylor, this is the Tai He Dian⑥. It was formerly used on such occasions as a new emperor's crowning, the emperor's birthday and the announcement of important edicts.

B: I can well imagine the solemn atmosphere of the scene. This hall is entirely different from any of the royal courts I have seen in the west. My hands are itching to take some snapshots of it as a remembrance of the visit. Do you think it is all right for me to do so?

A: Yes, of course. Go ahead.

B: Thank you. I've made it. Shall we proceed to the next hall?

A: Yes. Let's go on. This is the Zhong He Dian. It was here that the feudal emperors handled their daily affairs.

B: How splendid! A peaceful and tranquil atmosphere permeates the place.

A: The last of the three is Bao He Dian. It was built in the Ming Dynasty. Banquets and royal examinations were held here.

B: Thank you for your excellent explanation. I learned a lot about China.

A: It's my real pleasure.

5. Visiting the West Lake 游西湖

(A: Guest; B: Guide)

A: What a beautiful lake!

B: Yes. West Lake has been a scenic spot for hundreds of years. This scene is called "Autumn Moon over the Calm Lake". We can have a fine view of the moon from this platform in the evening.

A: You see, the green hills and clear water really provide magnificent scenery.

B: That's why people call West Lake a dazzlingly brilliant pearl.

A: Would you recommend some more scenic spots to see around West Lake?

B: Yes. There are ten most well-known scenic spots. They are known as "the Top Ten Views".

A: They are Snow Remnants on the Broken Bridge, Three Pools Mirroring the Moon, Twin Peaks Piercing to the Clouds, Lotus Breeze in the Winery Courtyard, Su Causeway in Spring Dawn, Viewing Fish at Flower Harbor, Evening Bell Chime from the Southern Screen Hill, Lei Feng Pagoda against the Sun Setting, Listening to the Orioles Singing in the Willows, and this Autumn Moon over the Calm Lake⑦.

B: All the names are so poetic. But our time is so limited.

A: Don't worry. We will have time to see most of them. Look, here we are at Three Pools Mirroring the Moon.

Notes 注释

① 杭州的灵隐寺之所以叫灵隐寺,是因为其开山祖印度惠理和尚认定此地的飞来峰为印度灵鹫峰飞来,是一处神灵隐居之地。

② 天王殿,也有译成"Heavenly Protectors' Hall"的。

③ 弥勒佛,佛教里的诸佛之一,一般被认为是未来佛,是西方极乐世界的教主。

④ 心宽体胖。

⑤ 韦驮,也叫韦驮天,是四大天王手下32大将之首。

⑥ 太和殿的通常译法为"the Hall of Supreme Harmony",下文中的中和殿为"the Hall of Central Harmony",保和殿为"the Hall of Preserving Harmony"。

⑦ 此为西湖旧十景,分别是:断桥残雪、三潭印月、双峰插云、曲苑风荷、苏堤春晓、花港观鱼、南屏晚钟、雷峰夕照、柳浪闻莺与平湖秋月。

Useful Sentences 必学句型

1. Are you ready to start?
   可以出发了吗?

2. Here we are at the entrance of…
   现在我们来到了……的门口。

3. We eagerly want to know the history of the temple. Could you give us some information about it?
   我们很想知道一些这个寺庙的历史,你能给我们讲一讲吗?

4. The whole trip takes about three hours.
   整个行程大约需要三小时。

5. According to our schedule, today we're going to visit…
   根据我们的行程,今天我们要去参观……

6. Take your time. I'll be waiting for you here.
   慢慢来,我会在这等你的。

7. I'm eager to see what they look like.
   我迫不及待地想看到它们是什么样的。

8. Let's move on.
   我们往前走。

9. Would you please wait for a moment? I am going to buy the tickets.
   请等会儿好吗? 我去买票。

10. Please meet at 11:00 by the gate.
    请于11点钟在大门口集中。

11. You can take some time to walk around, please be back to the bus at a quarter to 4 o'clock.

你可以自己去转转，请在3:45回到车上。

Passage Reading 阅读材料

General Yue Fei was a Song commander who led an army north against the Jin invaders when Hangzhou was the capital of the Southern Song Dynasty. Despite his success, he was ordered to withdraw by Emperor Gaozong on the advice of his Prime Minister, Qin Hui, who favored capitulation. Yue Fei was framed, arrested and killed along with his son, on the charge of some "probable" crimes.

Only 21 years later, Yue Fei was exonerated under the force of public opinion and buried with due ceremony. In 1221 a temple was also built to honor Yue Fei at Qixia Ridge. For generations, people have visited here to pay their respects to the hero who was determined to recover the lost territories. However, of all the sites in Hangzhou attacked during the "cultural revolution", Yue Fei's Tomb and Temple suffered the worst destruction. The clay statue of the general was smashed, steles written in his calligraphy were broken and stolen, and the kneeling iron-cast figures of the officials who framed Yue Fei disappeared. After the downfall of the "gang of four", local authorities moved quickly to restore the site in 1979 and today, the present temple, in some ways, surpasses the old.

Exercises 练习

1. **Reading and Translation**

As a popular saying goes, "there is a paradise above, so are there Hangzhou and Suzhou below". In the 13th century, Marco Polo came to Hangzhou and declared it to be "the finest, most splendid city in the world…where so many pleasures amy be found that one fancies oneself to be in the paradise".

The focus of the exceptionally beautiful city is West Lake. It is 3 miles across and 9 miles around, with islets and temples, pavilions and gardens, causeways and arched bridges, flowers and trees. All these have made Hangzhou's West Lake "a landscape composed by a painter".

There are two man-made causeways that divide West Lake into three parts. They are the Bai Causeway and the Su Causeway. Scenic and poetic, both of them are ideal stretches to walk on West Lake. The Bai Causeway was named after Bai Juyi, a famous poet in the Tang Dynasty, who fell into disfavor in the capital and was sent here to serve as a governor in 822-824 A.D. He was to the construction of the causeway, which was composed of the silt dredged from the lake.

2. **Complete the Following Dialogues in English with the hints given in Chinese**

(1) (A: Guide; B: Guest)

A: Good morning, sir.

B: Good morning. 今天天气真好，是不是？

A: Yes. 这天太适合出去游玩了。

B：_____？

A：首先，我要带你们去看一座著名的古塔。It's called Six Harmonies Pagoda.

B：六和塔？

A：An interesting name, isn't it? 我过会儿再跟你说为什么这么称呼。

B：All right. _____？

A：We will also 去参观个茶园。

B：That sounds interesting, too.

A：我想你们肯定会喜欢这两个地方的。

(2)（A：Guide；B：Guest）

A：Good morning, sir.

B：_____你说过今天我们要去坐船游西湖的，对不对？

A：Yes，我们第一个项目就是游西湖。

B：How great!

A：Now we will start our lake cruise soon. 我昨天跟大家讲过，杭州西湖原来是个泻湖。

B：而现在却是这么漂亮的一个湖。

A：Yes. 让我们一起来欣赏西湖美丽的风景吧。

B：What is the mound under the pavilion there?

A：_____, who has become the symbol of true love now.

B：What a beautiful arched bridge that is next to it!

A：_____

B：那边那条长堤是不就是你讲的白堤呀？

A：No. That is _____, which was built _____

B：现在能看到湖中的岛了，有好几个呢。

A：Yes, there are three. 最大的，也是最有名的一个叫_____

3. Role-play

Situation A

You are taking a Canadian group and having a tour to Lingyin Temple. Explain what you can see there to your guests.

Situation B

Some foreigners from an English spoken country have come to your college and they want to look around your campus. Show them around as a guide.

Unit 5　Dining at a Chinese Restaurant 用中餐

本课导读

俗话说"民以食为天",吃饭对中国人来说是头等大事。然而对来中国的游客来说,这就不仅是个果腹的问题,更重要的是一个学习的过程。因此,在中餐厅接待外国游客时,导游员除了带客人入座、帮客人点菜外,更要学会向客人介绍我们中餐所特有的东西,如菜的上法、吃法,菜的特点,文化背景等。甚至我们的餐具——筷子,也值得我们好好向老外介绍一番。

Special Terms　专业词汇

menu	菜单	braised	炖
cooking	烹饪	a course	一道菜
order	点菜	cold dish	冷盘
soft drink	软饮料	beggar's chicken	叫花鸡
lazy Susan	转盘	Dongpo pork	东坡肉
color	色	shrimps with Longjing tea leaves	
fragrance/aroma	香		龙井虾仁
flavor	味	ham	火腿
appearance	形	Sweet and Sour West Lake Fish	
cuisine	烹调风格;烹饪		西湖醋鱼
shred	丝	carp	草鱼
slice	片	weever	鲈鱼
cube	块	sturgeon	鲟鱼
dice	丁	yellow croaker	黄鱼
fried	煎	Mandarin fish	鳜鱼
stewed with brown sauce	红烧	fresh water eel	黄鳝
deep fried	炸	staple food	主食
stir-fried	炒	ginger	姜
boil	煮	garlic	蒜
steam	蒸	shallot	葱
roast	烤	leek	韭菜
smoked	熏	greasy	油腻的

minced	剁碎的	toothpick	牙签
bamboo shoot	笋尖	vegetable soup	蔬菜汤
bean curd	豆腐	sauté sliced fish in tomato sauce	
pickling	腌制		茄汁鱼片
lard	猪油	chef	主厨
assorted cold dish	什锦冷盘	recipe	食谱
chopsticks	筷子	seasoning	调料
hot pot	火锅	local flavor	风味食品
roast Beijing duck	北京烤鸭	tempting/inviting	令人开胃的
mushroom with green cabbage		ingredients	烹调原料
	冬菇菜心	green pepper	青椒
sweet-sour pork	古老肉	agaric	木耳

  Situational Conversations　情景对话

1. Greeting the Guests　迎客

Scene

（A：Waitress；B：Guide；C：Guest）

A：Good evening, ladies and gentlemen. Do you have a reservation?

B：I'm afraid not. Could you arrange a table for my guests now?

A：I'm sorry, the restaurant is full now. But if you would like to wait, you are more than welcome to do so.

B：How long do you think we will have to wait?

A：About ten minutes. Would you care to① have a drink in the lounge while waiting?

B：What do you think?

C：All right. Thanks a lot.

A：We can seat your party now. Will you please come with me? This way, please. Here is your table. Is it all right?

B：This table is too close to the toilet. Can I have another one?

A：Would you prefer a table by the corner?

B：I don't like that either. Is there a table available by the window? We'd like to have a night view of the city.

A：Let me check. Ah, you're so lucky, there's a table available now. Please move over there and be seated. The waiter will be here in a minute.

B：Thank you very much.

A：It's my pleasure.

2. Taking Order   点菜

Scene 1

（A: Guide; B: Guest）

A: Good evening, sir. Do you want me to get you something to drink while you look at the menu?

B: Yes, please. We'd like to try some Chinese beer. What brand do you recommend?

A: Tsingdao Beer is very popular in China. Would you like to try some?

B: OK. We will take two Tsingdao Beers, very cold, please.

A: Are you ready to order now, sir?

B: Yes. But this is our first visit to China. We love Chinese food, but to tell the truth, we know very little about it.

A: Well, there are eight main cuisines② in China, such as Cantonese food, Sichuan food and Zhejiang food…

B: How is Zhejiang food different from Sichuan food?

A: They are very different. Zhejiang food tends to be fresh and mild, while most Sichuan dishes are spicy and hot.

B: What about Cantonese food?

A: Cantonese food is light and known for its tenderness and freshness.

B: That sounds great, but can we order both of them?

A: Yes, Of course.

B: Let's have the Shelled Shrimps with Longjing Tea Leaves, please.

A: It's one of the famous dishes of Hangzhou. It looks nice both in shape and color; it is very delicious.

B: And also the Fish-Flavor Shredded Pork, please.

A: It is typical of Sichuan style.

B: Is it cooked with fish?

A: No. It has nothing to do with fish, but it is cooked with special fixings and condiments. So it tastes like fish.

B: Great! And here is a chicken and mushroom soup. Do you think the soup is tasty?

A: Yes. And I think that is enough for you. If you want anything else later, just call the waiter.

B: That's right! You're so considerate.

A: I hope you will enjoy your meal.

B: Thank you. We will.

Scene 2

（A: Guide; B: Customer）

A: Get seated, sir, and here is the menu.

B: Thank you.

A: Would you care for a drink before you order, sir?

B: Yes, beer please.

A: Yes sir. I'll get one for you. What are you going to take?

B: Well, let me see. Anything special for this restaurant?

A: They have plain sauté shrimps, fried boneless pork with sweet and sour sauce, and shredded beef in oyster oil,③ etc.

B: Very good.

A: These are our local specialties.

B: OK. We'll take them all.

A: Is there anything else you would like to have?

B: Please also ask them to bring us an assorted cold dish.

A: OK.

Scene 3

(A: Guide; B: Customer)

A: Good evening, ladies and gentlemen.

B: Good evening.

A: This way, please. This is our table. Is it all right?

B: This is fine.

A: What would you like to have?

B: This is our first trip to China. Will you recommend us some Chinese dishes?

A: Is there a maximum of your expense?

B: We don't care about money. We'd like to have some good dishes of Chinese characteristics.

A: OK. Let me see. Would you like shrimps with tomato, fried prawns, chicken cubes with egg white, sweet and sour boneless pork, sliced pork with pepper and ginger, fish slices with dregs of wine④, and fish balls soup? Six dishes and one soup, is that all right?

B: It sounds nice to me. Thank you.

A: How do you like these dishes?

B: We are doing fine. The dishes are colorful and tasty.

A: That's good.

B: How much altogether?

A: Let me get it for you. Here is the bill. The total amount is one hundred and eighty-five yuan.

B: Here is two hundred.

A: Thank you. And here is your change.

B: Thank you.

A: It's my pleasure.

3. Serving the Food 上菜

Scene

(A: Guide; B: Customer; C: Waitress)

A: Excuse me, sir. According to the specifications of Chinese food, we serve dishes first and then soup.

B: Very good, thank you.

A: Do you want some soup?

B: What soup do they have?

A: Let me check. They have "sliced chicken soup", "three kinds of slices soup"⑤, "dried mushroom clear soup", and so on.

B: May we have one "three kinds of slices soup", please.

A: OK. I'll ask the waitress to get it for you. Anything else?

B: Are there any refreshments?

A: Yes, there are assorted fried noodles, steamed mashed bean dumplings, and steamed shelled shrimps ravioli⑥, etc.

B: Fine! I want some assorted fried noodles, please.

A: All right. Here you are. Anything else?

B: No, thank you. I have had quite enough. Waitress, bring me the bill, please.

C: Here you are, sir.

B: Here is two hundred yuan. Keep the change, please.

C: We don't accept tips here. But thank you all the same.

B: Well, thank you very much indeed for the delicious meal.

C: Thank you for coming. Please call again. Good night.

B: Good night.

Notes 注释

① care 在此为"喜欢,愿意,想望"的意思,后跟 for something 或不定式。如:Would you care for a game of table tennis? 来打一局乒乓球好吗？I don't care for him to read this letter. 我不愿让他看这封信。I don't care to go there 我不愿到那儿去。

② 我国的八大菜系是四川菜系、山东菜系、广东菜系、江苏菜系、浙江菜系、福建菜系、湖南菜系和安徽菜系,简称川、鲁、粤、苏、浙、闽、湘、徽。

③ 这几道菜分别是清炒虾仁、糖醋里脊、蚝油牛柳。

④ 酒糟鱼片。

⑤ 三鲜汤。

⑥ 什锦炒面、豆沙包和虾肉馄饨。

Useful Sentences 必学句型

1. Could you arrange me a table now?
   能不能给我安排一张桌子？

2. Would you care to have a drink in the lounge while waiting?
   你要不要在休息室边等边喝点什么？

3. I'd like to have…
   我想要……

4. Is there anything else you would like to have?
   你还要什么别的吗？

5. Anything good for this evening?
   今晚有什么好吃的吗？

6. What would you like to have?
   你想要点什么？

7. Here is the bill. The total amount is…
   这是你的账单，一共是……

8. Here is your change.
   这是找你的钱。

9. May I take your order?
   可以点菜了吗？

10. What would you like to go with your steak?
    你的牛排配什么菜呢？

11. Could you give us a brief description of the Chinese food?
    你能不能大致给我们介绍一下中国菜？

12. Well, we have no idea of the food here. Can you recommend some to us?
    噢，我对这里的食物不太熟悉，你能为我们推荐几个吗？

Passage Reading 阅读材料

  In China, cooking is an art. Quite different from Western cooking where recipes are followed strictly like laboratory instructions, Chinese cooking always allows for a creative and stylistic touch to it. While in western cooking the recipe is the key to success in any culinary attempt, in Chinese cooking the experienced and well seasoned chef is the guarantee. That is why restaurants, but or small, would always boast of their chefs and advertise their dishes as well.

  "Colorful", "varied", "delicious" and "complex" are often used to describe Chinese food. Great attention is paid to aesthetic appreciation of the food because the food should be good not only in flavor and smell, but also in color and appearance.

  One of the very famous Chinese dishes, the Beggar's Chicken, is introduced as follows.

  Beggar's chicken is included in the menu for most banquets held in Hangzhou. The name of this dish sounds a little bizarre, for it is a beggar who stated this unique cooking method.

  A long time ago, a feudal emperor, escorted by a big party, took a ride out in the country. By the noon time, he felt very hungry. So he took a rest in a pavilion. The day was fine and there was a gentle breeze in the air. Suddenly, a pleasant smell came into his nostrils. He immediately ordered his men to track the smell. They found a beggar eating a chicken by a path. The beggar was brought to the emperor and sacrificed his chicken. The hungry emperor tasted it and was convinced he had never tasted any chicken as good as this. Later, when he returned to the capital, he asked the beggar to prepare the chicken for his daily meal and for loyal banquets as well.

  The way of preparing the chicken is simple. After the chicken is cleaned, it is wrapped in lotus leaves coated with clay. It is roasted in the fire for no less than four hours. Naturally, all the good fragrance of the chicken is contained right inside.

Exercises 练习

1. Reading and Translation

Chopsticks have been used in China for thousands of years. They are used either to grasp the food or to push it from plate to mouth. They are available for all purposes except eating soup or ice cream. Chopsticks are normally used in China, but you should not hesitate to ask for a knife or fork if you are embarrassed about your ability to eat with Chinese chopsticks. However, if you want to learn how to use chopsticks, your hosts will definitely help you with great patience. As days go by, you will be surprised at how quickly you will progress.

2. Complete the Following Dialogues in English with the hints given in Chinese

(1) (A: Waitress; B: Guide; C: Guest)

A: Good evening. 欢迎来到我们餐厅。

B: 晚上好。这是我的两个美国客人，他们想尝尝你们餐厅的特色菜。

A: _____?

B: 没，恐怕没有。有两个人的桌子吗?

A: I'm sorry. 目前没有空桌子。Would you please _____? 那边的桌子马上就要好了。

B: Do you mind 等一会儿?

C: No. Not at all.

A: The table over there _____ now. 请跟我来。

B: _____

(2) (A: Waitress; B: Guide; C: Guest)

A: Good morning, sir. 你们几个人?

B: 就他们俩。

A: _____? We have oolong tea, chrysanthemum tea and green tea.

B: What do you think? 我建议你们要绿茶吧。

C: All right. 我们就要绿茶。

A: What would you _____? We have 各种各样的点心。

C: Well, 我们对这里的食物不太熟悉。Can you _____?

B: 乐意为你效劳。

C: Thanks.

B: 小姐，结账。

A: 好的。一共168元。

C: _____

A: 这是找你的钱，32元。谢谢光临，欢迎下次再来。

3. **Role-play**

Situation A

You are a waitress in Lou Wai Lou Restaurant. One evening a foreign couple, who know very little about Chinese food come to the restaurant. Arrange a table for them and help them make their order by giving them recommendation.

Situation B

There are eight famous Chinese cuisines. Divide the class into eight groups and each is responsible for getting information of one cuisine as much as possible. A representative of each group is to make a presentation according to the class.

Unit 6 Visiting the Tea Garden
参观茶园

本课导读

茶叶是世界三大饮料之一，也是中国文化的重要组成部分。由于人们生活水平逐渐提高，对健康越来越关注，世界上喝茶的人也越来越多。杭州作为世界名茶龙井茶的原产地，其茶园早已成为国外游客了解茶叶、了解中国茶文化的必去之地。因此，作为杭州的导游，就必须了解一些茶叶的相关知识，特别是西湖龙井茶的独特之处及其整个生产、加工乃至品尝的细节。只有这样才能真正达到向国外游客介绍我国茶文化、我们西湖龙井茶的目的。

Special Terms 专业词汇

tea	茶	ferment	发酵
teapot	茶壶	chlorophyll	叶绿素
bulk tea	散茶	vitamin	维生素
tea set	茶具	black tea	红茶
tea ceremony	茶道	teahouse	茶馆
grind	磨	tea dust	茶沫
green tea	绿茶	tea tray/board	茶托
flower-tea	花茶	acidic	酸性的
jasmine-tea	茉莉花茶	alkaline	碱性的
oolong tea	乌龙茶	grade	等级
aroma	香味	process	加工
tea polyphenols	茶多酚	grease	涂脂于
tannin	丹宁	remove the excess fat	去油腻
tea plantation	茶园	detoxifying	解毒
prune	剪除	digestion	消化
household responsibility system	家庭责任制	beverage	饮料
sandy	沙质的	rainfall	降雨量
slope	斜坡	pH value	pH 值
humidity	湿度	drain	排水
brick tea	砖茶	dissolve	分解
the classic of tea	茶经	antiseptic	杀菌的
brew	泡茶	diabetes	糖尿病

hypertension	高血压	camellia	山茶
coronary heart disease	冠心病	herbal	中草药的
reduce weight	减肥	medicinal	医药的
tea basket	茶篓	antioxidant	抗氧化剂

Situational Conversations　情景对话

1. On the Way to the Tea Plantation　沿途

（A：Guide；B：Guest）

A：OK, ladies and gentlemen. Did you have a good walk in the temple area?

B：Yes, we did. We had good exercises. Are we going to walk more?

A：Not for the moment. Now, we are driving to visit something very special in Hangzhou.

B：What is it?

A：It's the world famous Dragon Well Tea^① plantation.

B：That's great. I've heard and read of it before I came to China. It is said that the Dragon Well Tea grown here is the best green tea in the world. But why is it so?

A：There are two reasons: the natural conditions and the special way of processing.

B：Can we have more details?

A：Of course. As you know, tea grows well in warm and humid climate. But it doesn't like too much water. This tea plantation or tea village provides an ideal condition for tea growing. It is a village in a valley which opens toward east to the largest river in this province. On the one hand, the tea bushes are protected from the cold northerly wind. On the other hand, the humidity from the river reaches here easily. And also, the soil here is sandy which drains well.

B：I see. What about the processing?

A：As for the processing. First of all, it's all done by hand. Secondly, it's a work of experience. We will see a demonstration of the processing later.

B：Thank you very much.

A：It's my pleasure.

2. At the Tea Plantation　在茶园

（A：Guide；B：Guest）

A：Ladies and gentlemen, attention please. Here we've come to the tea plantation. You can see rows of tea bushes on the terraces. Now, let's go to take a close look at the bushes.

B：How interesting. This is my first time to see tea bushes so closely. How long does one bush last?

A：The life of the tea bushes is around 75 years, during which, they are usually pruned twice with a 25-year interval.

B: Is tea a bush or a tree?

A: That is a good question. Tea is actually a tree. Those here are kept bushy by pruning and trimming, for the convenience of picking and better productivity.

B: I see. Talking about picking, how is it done?

A: Every leave is picked by hand. Actually, they only pick the tip of the new branches. Only those very tender shoots are picked.

B: How many times can they pick in a year?

A: There are three picking seasons: spring, summer and autumn. The bushes don't grow in winter therefore there is no picking. And the leaves picked in different times fall into different grades.

B: How?

A: Generally speaking, the spring leaves are the best, the autumn the second and the summer, the third. The tea picked before April 4 is the best among all, because that's usually the first picking in a year, which has a whole winter of nutrition accumulation.

B: How can a non-expert tell the grade?

A: First, he can do it by looking at the color. The lighter the better, because the younger leaves are in lighter color. Second, by looking at the size of the leaves. As long as the leaves are not broken, the smaller the better. Smaller also means younger. Third, by smelling. And fourth, by tasting.

B: I see. Thank you so much. I've learned a lot.

A: It's my pleasure. Now, let's go to see how it is processed.

3. By the Drying Oven 看炒茶

(A: Guide; B: Guest)

A: Ladies and gentlemen, here is how the Dragon Well Tea is processed. Please look at what this gentleman is doing. He is drying the tea leaves by hand.

B: Dear me! He seems to be frying vegetables with his hand! It must be very hot, because the leaves are steaming.

A: You are right. The whole drying process is done in two stages: drying and shaping. For the drying stage, the temperature is around 80 degrees centigrade. It lasts a quarter of an hour. For the second stage, the shaping, the temperature is about 30 degrees centigrade. It is about half an hour.

B: How much can he dry in a day for eight hours?

A: Just one kilogram. No more than 200 grams of fresh leaves are allowed for each time.

B: That's labour consuming. How many people are doing this job in this village?

A: There are 500 hundred families in this village and each family has one or two doing this teawork. The men in a family are obligated to do the job.

B: Why don't they use machines?

A: As our late premier Zhou Enlai said, Dragon Well Green Tea is not only a beverage, but also a form of art. If it is done by machine, it will not only lose the nutrition but also the artistic features due to the inflexibility of machine.

A: All right. That's a good reason. Now, this batch of tea is finished, right? Can we taste it?

B: Not this very batch. After being dried, the tea has to be kept with caustic lime[②] for about a week to get rid of the grassy smell before it is ready for drinking. But we can surely go inside to taste the ready tea. Let's go in.

A: Thank you very much for your good and detailed explanation.

4. At the Teahouse 在茶室

(A: Guide; B: Guest)

A: Good afternoon, ladies and gentlemen. Welcome to our tea village. Welcome to our teahouse. Please get seated.

B: Thank you. Is the tea in the cup ready for drinking?

A: Yes, but you'd better not drink it now. As you know, drinking tea is far more artistic than drinking other drinks. That's why there is tea ceremony.

B: That's right. But how?

A: The first low cup of tea is not for drinking but for checking the aroma. Swirl the glass and smell it. Do you get the special tea aroma?

B: Yes. Very freshening and pleasant.

A: Now, let's go to the second step by asking the girl to add more water into our cups. And this cup is for drinking.

B: Leaves keep getting into my mouth. Can I eat them?

A: Yes. Tea leaves are edible. If you eat the leaves, you get a hundred percent of the nutrition. If you just drink the water, you only get 30% of it.

B: If I don't eat the leaves, are they thrown away after this second step?

A: No. If you have time, you can have the third step. Refill your cup and this time use your eyes in stead of your mouth, look at the shape of the leaves. They look really delicate.

B: OK, please refill my cup. Ah yes. How beautiful they look.

A: While you are looking at the beautiful leaves in your cup, the real taste of the tea comes to your mouth. This is what we call after-taste.

B: Yes, you are right. How magic!

A: Not only does this tea have a special taste, but also high nutrition and good medicinal effect.

B: I would like to hear about it very much.

A: The Dragon Well Green Tea is rich in vitamins, chlorophyll, tea polyphenols and many other trace elements.

B: Yes?

A: They help people remove the excess fat, relief diabetes, prevent from getting coronary heart disease and even cancer.

B: How great! Can I buy some tea here?

A: Yes. I'm very glad to pack it for you.

B: Thank you so much for your taking us here to visit. This has been wonderful.

A: You are very welcome.

Notes　注释

① 龙井茶以色绿、香郁、味醇、形美"四绝"闻名中外。茶叶扁平挺秀、光滑匀齐、翠绿而略黄。泡在杯中，芽芽直立，汤色明亮，滋味甘鲜，被誉为"黄金芽"。龙井茶为绿茶，它与红茶及乌龙茶的最大的区别在于它是不经发酵的茶，而红茶和乌龙茶是发酵或半发酵的茶。

② 生石灰。

Useful Sentences　必学句型

1. It is said that...
   据说……

2. On the one hand, ...On the other hand, ...
   一方面……另一方面……

3. Talking about the picking, how is it done?
   说到采摘，茶叶是怎样采摘的？

4. Generally speaking, ...
   一般来说，……

5. Welcome to our tea village. Welcome to our teahouse. Please get seated.
   欢迎来到我们茶村，欢迎来到我们茶楼。大家请坐。

6. Can I buy some tea here?
   我可以在这买茶叶吗？

7. I'm very glad to pack it for you.
   我很乐意给你装罐。

8. This has been wonderful.
   这个（行程）太好了。

9. The village covers an area of 300 hectares, of which 30 are for tea production.
   村子占地 300 公顷，其中 30 公顷为茶园。

10. The drying process is done in two stages.
    炒制过程分两步进行。

11. You've been really informative. I have learnt a lot in this trip.
    你真是见多识广，这一程我学到了很多。

Passage Reading　阅读材料

What is the benefit of drinking tea? Well, drinking tea will not only quench thirst, overcome fatigue, but help digestion. Tea leaves, we know, contain some aromatic substances that can dissolve fat. It is said that a cup of tea would do good to one who has been stuffed with fat. Tea is known to be rich in various vitamins, notably Vitamin C. It is interesting to know that green tea contains five to six times more Vitamin C than black tea. That is perhaps why there has been an increasing demand for green tea in the world market. Scientific tests in recent years have discovered a new effect in drinking tea, i. e., radiation protection. This is attributable to the phenols in the contents of tea leaves which can absorb radioactive strontium.

Tea can also be used as an antiseptic. In the past, for instance, people in the remote areas in China would use tea to wash boils and wounds for sterilization and healing.

The way of drinking tea differs in different countries and regions. In Africa, for example, people often drink tea that is mixed with sugar or mint. Many Europeans add sugar or, milk to their tea. In China, too, herdsmen drink tea that is mixed with sheep or cow milk. The Han Chinese, however, prefer to drink what one might call plain tea, with its natural flavor.

Which is better, plain tea or tea that is mixed with sugar or mint or whatsoever? According to a national tea research center expert in Hangzhou, plain tea is distinctly better, for the mixing will reduce the medicinal or tonic value of the tea to a certain degree. But old habits die hard. Changing the age-old drinking habits is hardly possible. The time-honored tradition will linger forever.

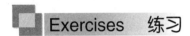
Exercises   练习

1. Reading and Translation

As tea drinking became more and more popular, the way of drinking tea varied. Before the Tang Dynasty, people were not particular about their tea drinking. They drank tea for thirsty and medical purposes. In the Tang Dynasty, people tended to have more delicate tea tastes. The process seemed complicated. The tea drinking usually had to go through several stages before he/she could perform the preparation process properly.

People in the Song Dynasty drank tea more delicately than those in the Tang. Tea drinking was very popular among royal families in the Tang. During the Song Dynasty there were teahouses in some cities. Common people could go and drink tea there.

People in the Ming Dynasty mainly drank green tea. Flower tea came into being in the Ming Dynasty.

Now, people who go to the teahouses are not really thirsty. Retired people go to the teahouse and sit there all day long to chat with each other. Sometimes, people bring guests to the teahouses. They chat, drink tea and eat many other snacks or dim sum.

Chinese people like to drink tea. It is the same with Western people who enjoy coffee. Tea was first produced in China, and it has been a part of daily life in China for at least 1500 years. Teahouses in China have always been the equivalent of the French cafes or the British pubs. Recently coffee shops and pubs have increased in Chinese cities, but there is no danger of them replacing teahouses.

2. Complete the Following Dialogues in English with the hints given in Chinese

(1) (A: Tour Guide; B: Guest)

A: Are we ready to go?

B: 刚参观了灵隐寺，我们都有些累了。What are we going to see next?

A: We are going to visit a tea plantation. 去那里不用走多少路，我们可以在那一边喝茶一边休息。

B: 那太好了，我正觉得渴了呢。What kind of tea are we going to drink?

A: _____

B: 我还没喝过绿茶呢。How is green tea different from black tea? 红茶我是喝过的。

A: Green tea 比红茶淡一些，它是没经过发酵的茶。

B: Fermented? 能给我们讲得细一点吗?

A: Black tea is totally fermented. 乌龙茶是半发酵茶，而龙井茶是不经发酵的绿茶。

B: I see. Thank you very much.

A: 不用客气。

(2)（A: Tour Guide; B: Guest）

A: Ladies and gentlemen, attention, please. 我们现在已经来到了龙井茶园。

B: 这里的空气多清新啊!

A: Yes. 看看你们的周围，全是绿色，能不清新嘛。

B: Are these tea bushes ready for picking?

A: 是的。你们知道哪一部分是采下来喝的吗?

B: No. We have no idea.

A: Only those tender shoots are picked. 所以春天是开采季节。

B: 茶树每年能采多久呀?

A: 春、夏、秋都可以采。但是春茶是一年中最好的。

B: So the tea picked now is the best, am I right?

A: 你说得很对。

B: Can we have a taste of the best tea in a year?

A: 当然。我们进去吧。

3. **Role-play**

Situation A

Give a five-minute presentation on Dragon Well Green Tea.

Situation B

You are by the tea-drying oven, in which a tea farmer is drying tea leaves, with a foreign-group. The group knows very little about the making of green tea. Try to explain the drying processing to your foreign guests.

Unit 7 Shopping at the Arts and Crafts Stores 工艺品店购物

本课导读

工艺品店购物是旅游活动中不可缺少的一个项目。在景点和沿途的讲解中，导游员一般会提及当地著名的工艺品，让游客对其有所了解。到达指定商店后，游客会自行挑选商品，然后询价，杀价，购买，付账等。作为导游，应做好翻译工作，以方便游客在游玩的闲暇中享受购物的乐趣。商品的价格通常是固定的，当客人要求打折时，导游应客气地作解释，安抚客人的情绪。

Special Terms 专业词汇

counter	柜台	ornaments	装饰品
stall/stand	售货摊	ring/finger ring	戒指
show window	橱窗	signet ring	印章戒指
show case	玻璃柜台	necklace	项链
shelf	货架	brooch	胸针
cash desk/cashier's desk	收银处	pendant	坠子
price tag	标价签	bracelet	镯子
fixed price	有定价	chain bracelet	手链
discount	打折扣	ear ring	耳环
change	零钱	trinket	小饰物
to keep the bill	留发票	safety-pin	别针
to wrap up	包装	cuff-link	袖扣
free of charge	不收费	diamond	钻石
to deliver	送	gold jewelries	金饰
be sold out/out of stock	售空	silver jewelries	银饰
shop assistant/salesman	售货员	pearl	珍珠
saleswoman	女售货员	imitation	仿制品
glassware counter	玻璃器皿部	genuine	真的
enamel ware	搪瓷器皿	fake	假的
jewelry/jewels	首饰, 珠宝	lacquer ware	漆器
jewel case	首饰盒	calligraphy	书法
antique/curio	古玩	ornament	装饰品

Unit 7 Shopping at the Arts and Crafts Stores 工艺品店购物

eardrop	耳坠	drawn work	抽纱
amethyst	紫水晶	brocade	织锦
crystal	水晶	lace	花边
carved lacquer ware	雕漆	straw ware	草编
porcelain	瓷器	woven rattan articles	藤编
pottery	陶器	rush products	蒲制品
shell carving	贝雕	silk fan	绢扇
egg-shell china	薄胎瓷	sandalwood fan	檀香扇
silk painting	绢画	snuff bottle	鼻烟壶
batik	蜡染画	bamboo scrolls	竹帘画
palace lantern	宫灯	silk flower	绢花
double-sided embroidery	双面绣		

Situational Conversations 情景对话

1. Buying Porcelain 买瓷器

(A: Salesman; B: Tourist)

B: Excuse me. What do you call this?

A: You have made a good choice, madam. This is called egg-shell china.

B: Oh, I see. I have seen it in my friend's room.

A: It is the porcelain of best quality[①], made in Jingdezhen.

B: Yes, I know it. Isn't it called "the capital of porcelain"?

A: Yes, madam. It is not for use, but for show.

B: China's goods are always unique. How much is it?

A: One set with 12 animals' symbol costs 260 yuan.

B: Oh, it is too expensive. Can't you offer a discount?

A: Sorry, madam. You know, it is known to be "as white as jade and as thin as paper".[②]

B: But I am afraid... Oh, It is of perfect Chinese traditional design, isn't it?

A: Yes, indeed.

B: Then, I will take one set.

2. Buying Teapot 买茶壶

(A: Salesman; B: Tourist)

A: Can I help you?

B: I want to find something typically Chinese to decorate my room.

A: How about this artistic tapestry[③] and this cloisonné vase?

B: Well, I am looking for something a little different. These teapots are beautiful. The color is similar to that of my sitting room. Are they made of porcelain?

A: No, they are made of clay. They are Yixing purple clay teapots. This kind of tea ware is very famous in China.

B: Ah, I see. How can I make tea with this teapot?

A: That depends on what kind of tea you want to make, the Chinese tea is classified into green tea, white tea, oolong tea, black tea, pu'er tea, scented tea and etc.. What kind of tea do you like?

B: Well, I am a little familiar with black tea. Can you show me how to make the tea?

A: I am sorry to say we do not have any tea in this shop, but I can tell you the steeping method. First, put the tea leaves into the pot, then put hot water into it, the amount of tea in proportion to④ water is 1 to 9. The temperature of the water is 100℃. After 10 seconds, the tea is ready.

B: Ah, I see. What is the price of this tea set?

A: It is 600 yuan.

B: That's too much, I will take it if you give me a 60% discount.

A: Well, I can just take 100 yuan off the price.

B: All right, I will take this set.

A: Anything else for you?

B: Yes, what is the design of this paper cut?

A: They are lotus flowers.

B: Ah, how beautiful! How much is it?

A: It is 20 yuan.

B: I will take it, can I have it framed? I want hang it up in the bedroom.

A: Yes, but you will have to pay for the frame. It is 30 yuan.

B: All right. Here is the money. It is 550 yuan altogether.

A: Thank you.

B: Would you give me a shopping bag?

A: Yes, here you are.

3. Buying Chinese Traditional Paintings 买中国画

(A: Saleswoman; B: Sandy; C: Tour Guide)

A: Good morning, what can I do for you?

B: Good morning. I want to look around first.

A: Shall I show you around and explain the antiques for you?

B: Thanks a lot. What are these?

A: These are old coins of Tang Dynasty.

B: Ah, I see. And what is this?

A: It is lacquer screen with Chinese traditional paintings. Do you like it?

B: Yes, I like it, but I'd like to buy some paintings. Do you have good ones?

A: Yes. How about these ones? These are landscapes and these are flower-and-bird paintings.

Unit 7 Shopping at the Arts and Crafts Stores 工艺品店购物

B: They are beautiful. The horses in this picture are living. Who painted it?

A: Xu Beihong. He was one of the most famous painters in China.

B: Is it genuine?

A: No, it is fake. The real one is very expensive. All our reproductions are marked and priced. Their prices are very reasonable.

B: How much is it?

A: It is 500 yuan.

B: That is too much. I was born in 1954. My Chinese friend said that I was born in the year of horse. That is why I like this painting most.

A: All right, this can be marked down 20%.

B: I won't take it until it is marked down 30%.

A: You are a good bargainer. All right, that is 350 yuan.

B: Can I have it shipped to the United States?

A: Certainly, but you will have to pay for the postage.

B: How much will the postage be?

A: About 80 yuan.

B: This is the address. Please mail it to this address and this is the money, 430 yuan.

A: Thank you, here is your receipt.

B: Thank you.

4. Buying Carpet 买地毯

(A: Salesman; B: Tourist)

A: Welcome!

B: How marvelous the weaving articles!

A: We deal with products from several well-known carpet factories in China. This carpet is hand-made by traditional ways.

B: Is this hand-made one?

A: No, this carpet is made by machine.

B: This must be silk rug, it looks gorgeous.

A: Absolutely right. They are silk rug. You can enjoy the beautiful pattern carefully.

B: This tapestry's pattern is quite modern.

A: Yes. Many visitors are fond of such pattern. It is no woolens and silk, but synthetic fabrics.

B: Very nice. If you hadn't told me, I would not have noticed any diffierence.

A: They are lighter, cheap and mothproof.

B: How much is this small rug?

A: 380 yuan.

B: Sounds good. I'd like to buy it as a souvenir and put it in my bedroom.

5. Buying Light Handicrafts 买轻便手工艺品

(A: Salesman; B: Tourist)

A: What can I do for you?

B: I plan to buy some handicrafts as souvenirs for my family and relatives.

A: We have quite a wide variety of handicrafts here. What do you have in mind?

B: I'd like something typical Chinese, but not very expensive. What is your advice?

A: I guess you are a tourist. You don't want anything too heavy, do you?

B: No. I want something light and easy to carry.

A: What about some papercuts? They will be a good present for girls. This set of 12 Chinese Animals is one of our best-selling items.

B: They are cute. I will buy one for my little niece.

A: Would you please come this way, miss? I'd like to show you some cloisonné articles.

B: They are beautiful, but must be quite expensive.

A: Not exactly. The earrings are 80 yuan a pair, and these bracelets are only 99 yuan a pair.

B: Are they? I will choose a pair of bracelets and a pair of earrings. I am sure my younger sister will be very glad to have them.

A: Anything else?

B: Yes, I'd like have a look at the shirts over there.

A: Sure. They are pure cotton.

B: I like this one. I will take three. I guess that's it. How much does it come to?⑤

A: Let me figure it out. That amounts to 565 yuan. May you be happy everyday.

Notes 注释

① of best quality   质量上乘
② as white as jade and as thin as paper   白如玉，薄如纸
③ artistic tapestry   艺术挂毯
④ in proportion to   与……成比例
⑤ How much does it come to?   共计多少钱？

Useful Sentences 必学句型

1. You want to buy some Chinese silk and satin, don't you?
   您想买些中国绸缎，是吗？

2. Is it made of pure Chinese silk?
   它是纯粹中国丝织的吗？

3. It's velvety and the colour is brilliant.
   它柔软光滑而且颜色鲜艳。

4. Is the colour fast?
   不褪色吗？

Unit 7 Shopping at the Arts and Crafts Stores 工艺品店购物

5. You can only wash it in lukewarm water.
   您只能在温水中洗。

6. What's the width?
   门幅多少?

7. It's two feet and four inches wide.
   宽二英尺四英寸。

8. I want to make a Chinese fashion coat. How many feet should I buy?
   我要做一件中式上衣,应买多少?

9. Let me take a measurement and calculate.
   让我量一量,计算一下。

10. Seven feet will be enough.
    七英尺就足够了。

11. By the way, what is the brand?
    顺便问一下,是什么牌子?

12. It is well received the world over.
    它在世界各地很受欢迎。

13. How much would that come to?
    总共要多少钱?

14. There is the satin suitable for making cushion covers there.
    那里有适宜做垫套的缎子。

15. I think the pink one is quite good.
    我看那粉红色的很好。

16. Ask the shop assistant to cut a pair for us.
    要店员给我们剪一对。

17. Don't you think we could use one to decorate our room?
    难道你不想买一条来装饰我们的房间吗?

18. Artistic tapestry is the highest form of expression of the rug weaving art, an exquisite handicraft of superb artistry in typical Chinese style.
    艺术挂毯体现了地毯纺织艺术的最高水平,是具有典型中国风格的手工艺精品。

19. Is this the marvellous landscape in Guilin?
    挂毯上是不是美丽的桂林山水?

20. What a lovely tapestry!
    多美的挂毯啊!

21. Which do you prefer, the linen one, the figured dacron or the brocade?
    您要哪种台布,亚麻的、提花涤纶还是织锦缎的?

22. You haven't anything cheaper, have you?
    你们没有再便宜一点儿的吗?

23. What fine needlework!
    多好的绣工啊!

24. The background is pale blue with traditional Chinese paintings of flowers and birds.
    底色是浅蓝的，还有中国花鸟画。

25. Can you pack the vases and send them to New York by mail for me?
    你替我把花瓶包装好寄往纽约，行吗？

26. They are made from different materials—dolomite, tough silk, organdie etc.
    它们是用不同的材料做的，白云石、绢、蝉翼纱等。

27. This is made of wild goose feather and this is made of skylark feather.
    这把是用雁毛做的，这把是用云雀毛做的。

Passage Reading 阅读材料

Specialties along the Yangtze

From Chongqing to Shanghai, the world's 3rd largest river covers an area of around 1.8 million square kilometers. Not only it features extraordinary scenery, but also it carries a long history and rich unique local products, crafted or natural. Many of these products could be ideal choice of souvenirs and gifts for foreign visitors.

Usually, westerners are more keen on those "typical" Chinese goods, such as silk, tea, jade, embroidery, porcelain, carpet, cloisonné and antiques, etc, although more and more people come to China for more general stuff. Some people visit China just for shopping, from clothing to bathroom paper rolls. Some people we know spent thousands of dollars and shipped life-sized terra-cotta soldiers back home.

Many of the items along the Yangtze have won high reputations, such as bamboo crafted items and Shu style embroidery in Chongqing; colorful Three Gorges stones in the Yangtze Three Gorges; turquoise stone in Wuhan; Jingdezhen porcelain (near Mt. Lu); Maofeng tea and four treasures in study in Huangshan; lacquer ware in Jingzhou (Shashi) and Yangzhou; silk in Suzhou, Zhenjiang and Shanghai; Su embroidery in Suzhou; clay figurines in Wuxi; jade in Shanghai and Yangzhou.

Following names are listed among best Chinese teas: Longjing (Hangzhou), Biluochun (Jiangsu), Huangshan Maofeng (Anhui), Junshan Silver Needle (Hunan), Qimen black tea (Anhui). They are all produced in Yangtze valley and best gift candidates.

Bargaining is normally acceptable in most of the shops except in department stores. Many of our customers feel bargaining is fun and could save a lot. Depends on the goods you are interested to buy or how strong a desire to buy it, 20% to 70% off the prices is where you can start your haggling. Why? You are a tourist! China is no exception.

For the expensive items, please keep the purchase receipts since you may be asked to produce them by customs when leaving China, and entering the customs of your own country.

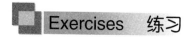

1. Reading and Translation

Canada contains huge metropolis, which are a reflection of the modernity and the wealth of this country, of the progress that over a few short centuries the conquerors from the Old World were able to initiate and develop in the cold lands of North America.

In spite of the fact that generations of settlers have transformed the landscape into a modern and comprehensive infrastructure system, Canada also remains the domain of nature, unspoiled, uncontested and dominating.

Here, perhaps more than in any other corner of the planet, nature is capable of arousing amazement, bewilderment and fascination, even to the most technocratic of human beings. The forces of nature manage and create phenomena that are decidedly unnatural, like rivers that run in the opposite direction, going back up their own sourse.

This unusual spectacle is called tidal bore and is due to one of the most powerful attractions that nature is able to unleash that between the sun and the moon which gives rise to the phenomenon of the tides.

2. Complete the Following Dialogues in English with the hints given in Chinese

(1) (A: Salesgirl; B: Tourist)

A: _____

B: 我想买中型淡蓝色底的景泰蓝花瓶。

A: _____

B: 哦, 我明天要离开中国, 没有时间啦。

A: _____

B: 让我看看, 大的价格如何?

A: _____

B: 很公道, 能给我看一下吗?

A: _____

B: 很漂亮, 我买一对, 相信我妻子会喜欢的。

A: _____

B: 你能把花瓶包起来并邮寄到纽约吗?

A: _____

B: 好的, 我该付多少钱?

A: _____

B: 好吧, 给你钱。

(2) (A: Salesgirl; B: Tourist)

A: _____

B: 是的, 我想给朋友买些礼物。

A: _____

B: 太好啦! 你们有黄金饰品吗?

A: _____

B: 我可以看一下吗?

A: _____

B: 非常漂亮, 就要它。

A: _____

B：可以看一下那个钥匙圈吗？
A：_____
B：很漂亮，给我 10 个像这样的。我相信这对我加拿大的朋友来说是些好礼物。

3. **Role-play**

Situation A

Suppose the tour member intends to buy a carpet for his friend. When the tour member arrives at the carpet factory, the salesman tries his best to make a detailed introduction to his products in order to sell his products at favorable price. However, the tour member begins to bargain for the carpet.

Situation B

One tourist plans to buy some souvenirs for his family members, but it is hard for her to decide what sort of souvenirs she should buy. At that moment, the salesman comes to promote his products and try to persuade her to buy Chinese traditional paintings.

Unit 8 Visiting the China Silk Museum and the Silk Factory
参观中国丝绸博物馆和丝绸厂

本课导读

丝绸是世界上最好的衣料之一，其优越性几乎没有其他原料可以匹敌。中国在四千五百多年以前就开始生产丝绸，是世界上最早开始生产丝绸的国家。而浙江是中国最大的丝绸生产地，中国丝绸博物馆就建在杭州。因此，参观丝绸博物馆和丝绸厂是杭州旅游的一个重要组成部分。与参观茶园一样，参观丝绸博物馆和丝绸厂也是一个了解中国文化的过程。在参观过程中，导游员不仅要向客人介绍丝绸的生产过程及丝绸的优越性，还要向他们介绍我们的丝绸历史、丝绸文化。同时，还要教客人如何鉴别丝绸的质量，识别真假丝绸等。

Special Terms 专业词汇

silk	蚕丝	loom	提花机
cocoon	蚕茧	brocade	织锦
sericulture	养蚕业	nylon	尼龙
pupa /chrysalis	蚕蛹	synthetic	合成的
larva	幼虫	silk scarf	丝绸围巾
fabric	布料	think silk	绢
satin	绸缎	silkworm	蚕
silkworm moth	蚕蛾	silkworm rearing house	蚕房
gauze	纱	silk floss	丝绵
filament length	丝长	silk floss quilt	丝绵被
sericin	丝胶	cushion cover	衬垫套
mulberry tree	桑树	dry cleaning	干洗
rearing net	蚕网	iron press	熨
silkworm egg	蚕卵	wring	拧，绞
cocoon sorting	选茧	thread	丝线
twin pupae/double cocoon	双宫茧	fiber	纤维
reeling	缫丝	bed spread	床罩
spool	线轴	wall hanging	墙帷
weave	织造	embroidery	刺绣
spinning	纺纱	graph paper	图纸

weft	纬线	quilt cover	被套
warp	经线	jacquard	提花织物
rayon	人造丝	printing and dying	印染
shuttle	梭子	bleach	漂洗

 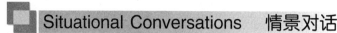

Situational Conversations 情景对话

1. On the Way to the Silk Museum 去丝绸博物馆的路上

(A: Guide; B: Guest)

A: Good afternoon, ladies and gentlemen. There is a saying for Hangzhou: up in heaven there is a paradise, down on earth, there are Suzhou and Hangzhou. Part of the reason is it is rich in local products, such as tea, silk and so on.

B: Yes, a friend of mine visited here last year and she went to a silk museum and a silk factory, where she had a wonderful time. Do we have a chance to do that?

A: That's exactly what I've planned for you to do this afternoon.

B: That's great. Thank you.

A: We'll pay a visit to the China Silk Museum[①] first of all to learn something about the sericulture in China and then we'll see how silk is produced in a silk factory.

B: That I'm sure will be very interesting. We know that China started making silk the earliest in the world. But could you tell us how early?

A: You are right. China is the first producer of silk in the world. More than 4 500 years ago, silk production was started in China, and our province soon became a major center.

B: In the museum, can we see the silk worms?

A: Yes, but few. Silkworm breeding is done by the farmers in the rural areas. It requires exceptional skill because the worms grow rapidly and are easily affected by changes in temperature and other factors.

B: I see. What is the life of a silkworm like?

A: The life cycle of silkworm is, let's say, from egg to ant, then to worm, to chrysalis in cocoon, and to moth who lays eggs. It is around 30 days.

B: Thank you. What do the silkworms live on[②]?

A: They live on mulberry tree leaves which grow abundantly here.

2. At the China Silk Museum 在丝绸博物馆

(A: Guide; B: Guest)

A: Ladies and gentlemen, may I have your attention, please. Here we are arriving at the silk museum. The first part of the museum was opened to the public in 1992. It is the first museum of this kind in China as well as the largest silk museum in the world.

B: Let's go in. I can't wait to see it.

Unit 8 Visiting the China Silk Museum and the Silk Factory   参观中国丝绸博物馆和丝绸厂

A: The museum collects and displays silk products of past generations and traditional silk production tools of various nationalities.

B: What a big museum!

A: Yes. It occupies five hectares, and has a floor space of 8 000 sqm and an exhibition space of 3 000 sqm. It contains eight different exhibition halls: the Prelude Hall, the Relics Hall, the Folk Custom Hall, the Silkworm Hall, the Silk Manufacturing Hall, the Weaving Hall, the Dyeing Hall, and the Achievement Hall.

B: So, here we can experience the 5000-year development of silk in a couple of hours.

A: That's right. What we first see is an old weaving apparatus on which you may try to weave silk yourselves, learning how silk was manufactured in the old times.

B: That must be great fun. Let me try.

A: Now let's move on. Exhibited here are silk production artifacts from the Neolithic Age. This piece of silk fabric exhibited here is tested to be more than 4000 years old.

B: How incredible.

A: China National Silk Museum all the while pays much attention to friendly cultural exchanges about silk with any other countries. With past years' efforts, the museum has been gradually developing to a high-standard research, collection, and authentication center of the ancient Chinese silk cloth.

B: That is really important. Can we walk around on our own?

A: Yes, of course. I'd like to give you 20 minutes for your own exploration now.

B: Thank you very much. See you later.

3. At the Silk Factory   在丝绸厂

(A: Guide; B: Guest)

A: Good afternoon, ladies and gentlemen. Now we are approaching the silk factory. It will be a bit noisy. So get prepared.

B: Look at all those cocoons. What are they doing with them there?

A: They are sorting. As you know, not all the cocoons are in good quality. Some are pierced, some are crushed, some have yellow secretion on the surface and some are twin pupae cocoons.

B: I don't see any thread on the cocoon. How they get it out?

A: You don't see the thread because it's all stuck together by the sericin produced by the silkworm while spinning. That's why the cocoons have to be boiled before they go to the reeling process[③].

B: I see. But why are there six or seven cocoons staying together?

A: The thread from one cocoon is so thin that it takes that many to make one fiber. Six or seven threads are twisted together while being taken out from the cocoons.

B: Ah ha! From here on, it's easier to understand. But how long can be the thread from one cocoon?

A: The length of the thread from a cocoon ranges from 800 to 1 000 meters.

B: Thank you. Just now you mentioned the twin pupae cocoons or double cocoons. What do they do with them?

A: That's a good question. Those cocoons are not good for reeling purpose because two threads are mixed together. But they are not a waste. They will be made into silk floss quilt. Now let's go to see how it works out.

B: Come and look here! All those twin pupae cocoons are soaked here.

A: Yes. When soaked long enough, the cocoons can be opened by hand and stretched. They put the stretches layer after layer to be a quilt. That's what they are doing over there. Let's go and see.

B: How nice it feels. It's soft and spongy. It must be really comfortable. Do they sell their products here?

A: Yes. Let me show you there.

4. At the Silk Fabric Counter 在丝绸柜台

(A: Guide; B: Guest)

A: OK, here is the shop. There are many selections. You can shop till you drop[④].

B: I'm looking for a silk shirt for my husband. Would you show me some, please?

A: Certainly. We have a wide selection of silk shirts here. But what size, please?

B: Large.

A: How do you like these?

B: How nice! They all look beautiful. But the problem is that I'm not good at choosing. I wonder if you could help me.

A: Yes, with pleasure. By feeling them, I can assure you that these shirts are fine quality. They are made of real silk with superb texture. I would recommend the purple one. It is the fashionable color this year. I'm positive that your husband would be grateful to you for such an excellent gift.

B: Thank you very much. Incidentally, is the color fast[⑤]?

A: Yes, it is and it is washable. But I would suggest that you wash it in lukewarm water. Please don't rub. Just use soapy water and rinse well.

B: Right then, I would like to buy it. How much is it?

A: The price tag says two hundred and eighty Yuan.

B: That is more than I expected to pay. Shall we look for a cheaper one of the same quality?

A: I'm afraid not. I hear from the lady that they are sold out. In my opinion, it is worthwhile for its quality, though a bit too expensive. It makes[⑥] a good gift for your husband. But anyway, you have all the right to make your own decision.

A: In that case, I might as well take it. Would you please go upstairs with me for something else?

B: Sure. Let's go.

Unit 8　Visiting the China Silk Museum and the Silk Factory　参观中国丝绸博物馆和丝绸厂

Notes　注释

① 中国丝绸博物馆位于杭州西子湖畔，是第一座全国性的丝绸专业博物馆，也是世界上最大的丝绸博物馆。占地五公顷，建筑面积8 000平方米，陈列面积3 000平方米，于1992年2月26日正式对外开放。
② live on　以……为主食，靠……为生。
③ 丝绸生产过程中在缫丝之前要进行煮茧，其目的就是将蚕茧上的丝胶煮掉，这样就能抽出丝线。
④ shop till you drop　买个够。类似的有eat till you drop, drink till you drop等。
⑤ fast　意为不褪色的。
⑥ make　是成为或变成的意思。如 she will make a good wife.

Useful Sentences　必学句型

1. Do we have a chance to do that?
   我们能不能这样做？

2. We'll pay a visit to…
   我们要参观……

3. I can't wait to see it.
   我等不及想看到它。

4. We can experience the 5000-year development of silk in a couple of hours.
   我们能在几个小时里体验五千年的丝绸发展史。

5. Walk around on our own.
   我们自己转转吧。

6. There are many selections. You can shop till you drop.
   这里有很多品种，你可以尽情买个够。

7. I wonder if you could help me.
   我想你能不能帮帮我。

8. That is more than I expected to pay.
   我不想为此付那么多钱。

9. I'm looking for a silk shirt for my husband. Would you show me some, please?
   我在给我先生找一件丝绸衬衫，能不能请你给我几件看看？

10. In that case, I might as well take it.
    这样的话，我还是要它吧。

11. Exhibited here are…
    这里展出的有……

12. How many yards must I buy to make a shirt?
    我要做一件衬衫得买几码布？

Passage Reading 阅读材料

Silkworms are delicate creatures. They can be easily kicked by rats, mosquitoes, and flies, or by the dust on the mulberry leaves. That is why the cat is a familiar scene in every silkworm village. That is also why farmers will lime wash the rearing houses before the breeding season sets in, and will sometimes clean the mulberry leaves one by one before they feed them to the worms.

Silkworms are hungry creatures, too. They eat a lot. In fact, they have to be fed every four hours, including at night. Female silk farmers are said to take as much care of silkworms as they do their own babies. Hence silkworms are given the intimate name "delicate babies". Now as they eat a lot, they drop a lot. The droppings of the silkworms make an excellent fertilizer, which is far superior to many chemical ones.

Silkworms are heavy sleepers by nature. They keep eating the leaves for a couple of days and then go to a long sleep, each of which lasts about 24 hours. When they wake up from a sleep, they plunge into eating the leaves with a better appetite than before. The last sleep is the longest sleep-about 36 hours or even longer. When they wake up, they are ready to spin cocoons. To show their readiness to spin, the worms will raise their fore legs, not the hind ones. Then the farmers will pick them up one by one from where they stay, which is usually a bamboo tray, and put them onto a straw mountain. It is not a real mountain, just straw arranged like the spikes of a wheel. The farmers have to see to it that no two silkworms stay too close to each other; otherwise, they are likely to make one cocoon instead of two and the silk threads will all get mixed up and serve no reeling purposes. The spinning process extends 3 to 4 days.

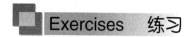 **Exercises** 练习

1. **Reading and Translation**

Now what happens is that the glutinous stuff that comes out of the mouth of a fully-grown silkworm is a long, long thread which goes round and round the worm, glued together. At the beginning, one will see a thin film of silk thread through which the worm is visible. When the spinning process is over, the cocoon is made, and the worm is wrapped inside, invisible.

When the cocoons are made, the farmers will pick them up and put them into bamboo baskets. Then they will transport them to the purchasing centers set up by the silk companies right in the rural areas. There, heating has to be done in good time to all the cocoons in order to kill, or rather, stifle the chrysalises inside. If they fail to do this, the worms will transform themselves from chrysalises into moths and emerge out of the cocoons, rendering them useless for reeling purposes with a hole in each of them.

2. **Complete the Following Dialogues in English with the hints given in Chinese**

(1) (A: Guide; B: Guest)

A: 那么, 这些就是蚕茧了, aren't they?

B: Yes, they are.

A: _____?

Unit 8 Visiting the China Silk Museum and the Silk Factory 参观中国丝绸博物馆和丝绸厂

B：They are sorting out the bad ones.

A：哪些是不好的茧？

B：Look carefully. You can see 并不是所有的茧都是高质量的。有些是 pierced, some are 压坏的, some 表面有黄色的分泌物, and some are 双宫茧。

B：I see. So those are the ones to be picked out?

A：Yes, 要不然丝绸的质量就会下降。

B：How interesting! _____?

A：They go to the reeling process.

B：我们会去看吗？

A：Yes, let's go now.

（2）（A：Saleswoman；B：Guest）

A：Good afternoon, Madame. 欢迎光临，需要帮忙吗？

B：我在给我先生找一件丝绸衬衫。Can you show me some, please?

A：Certainly. We have 很多丝绸衬衫可以挑选。But what size, please?

B：Large.

A：你喜欢这些吗？

B：How nice! They all look beautiful. 但问题是我不善于挑选。不知道你能不能帮我选一选。

A：Yes, with pleasure. I would 推荐那件紫色的，这是今年的流行色。

B：Thank you. I think this will fit my husband well. _____?

A：It's 250 yuan.

B：能不能便宜点？

A：I'm sorry, Madame. Our prices are fixed.

B：OK. 我要这件了。Here is 300 yuan.

A：这是找你的钱。Thank you.

B：Thank you. Goodbye.

3. Role-play

Situation A

You are the local guide of Mr. and Mrs. Ashmore. They want to buy some silk things in Hangzhou. But they don't know where to buy them and how to choose. You take them to a silk store and give them some advice as to what to choose.

Situation B

Mr. and Mrs. White, who are from Canada, are very interested in museums. Show them around the Zhejiang Provincial Museum. Try to explain to them as much as you can.

Unit 9 Handling Complaints 处理投诉

本课导读

旅游业是个涵盖面最广的服务业之一，它包括生活的方方面面。因此，在提供服务的过程中，由于种种原因，投诉和表扬一样在所难免。问题的关键在于如何处理好顾客的投诉。在遇到投诉时，首先要认真地、有礼貌地听完客人的抱怨，除非十分必要，否则不去打断他。听完以后要作出简单的重复以示理解无误，同时进行明确的道歉。可能有时要做投诉记录，然后决定由谁来处理问题。自己能直接解决的就直接解决。要是问题严重，需上级领导解决的，要向客人作出说明，并及时安排客人与领导见面。

Special Terms 专业词汇

reputation	信誉	encounter	遭遇到
unexpected circumstance	出乎意料的情况	unfriendly	不友好的
precaution	预防	unwilling	不愿意的
unfavorable	令人不快的	irresponsible	不负责任
expectation	期望	check sth. out	查某事
supportive and helpful	支持的，有帮助的	irritate	激怒
discomfort	不适	misplace	放错地方
upset	生气	get in touch with	与……取得联系
confronted with problem	遇到问题	be in charge of	主管
cope/deal with	处理	valuable	贵重物品
cancel	取消	in case	以防
delay	延误	suspect	怀疑
berate	严厉指责	uncaring	不关心的
reject	拒绝	overcharge	过高收费
complain about	对……投诉	in the strongest terms	最强烈地
complaint	投诉	object to	反对
sincere apology	真诚的道歉	dirty/filthy	肮脏的
misunderstanding	误解	investigate	调查
take action	采取行动	assure	保证
handle/settle a complaint	处理投诉	demanding	苛求的
incident	事件	sympathy	同情
frustration	恼怒	remedy	补救，赔偿

win-win	双赢	refund	退钱
lose	丢失	compensate for	赔偿
be missing	不见了	messy	凌乱的

Situational Conversations   情景对话

1. Missing Luggage   丢失行李

(A: Tour Guide; B: Guest)

B: Excuse me, is this all the luggage?

A: Yes, I think so.

B: My luggage seems to be missing.

A: How many pieces do you have?

B: Two. A large red hard-cover one and a small dark blue one. Both have wheels.

A: Could I see your luggage claim checks①?

B: Yes, here you are.

A: May I have your full name?

B: John Smith.

A: Just a moment. I'll check it out for you. Well, Mr. Smith, your luggage seems to have been misplaced.

B: What am I supposed to do? They have all my things.

A: I'm terribly sorry. We'll get in touch with the airline and try our best to get them back as soon as possible. Please fill out this claim form with your check number.

B: OK. What will happen if you can't find them?

A: Well, Mr. Smith, I do not work for the airline. Let me get a representative from the airline to speak with you. He or she can answer your questions more completely.

B: My vacation is ruined! I'm sure I'll never see my luggage again!

A: Please, Mr. Smith, let's talk to an airline official.

B: All right. Let's do it right now.

2. An Angry Tourist   愤怒的游客

(A: Guide; B: Guest)

A: You asked to see me, Mr. Smith?

B: I certainly did. I'm not at all happy.

A: What seems to be the problem, Mr. Smith? How can I help you?

B: You can help me by getting my bathroom put right. It's in an absolutely terrible condition. When I tried the shower, no water came out at all. I'm wondering why they put me in such a room. They should have known its condition before we arrived.

A: I am sorry to hear that. There must have been a mistake. I'll have it fixed immediately.

B: That's not all. There's no soap, towels or toilet paper!

A: I sincerely apologize for this, Mr. Smith. I think the hotel is rather short-staffed[2] at present. The housekeeping staff should have checked your room. I'll attend to it as soon as possible.

B: Don't bother[3]. I'm not happy with this room for some other reasons, too. Look, it isn't a twin room as I booked. Besides, this room faces the street, it is rather noisy. Could you help me change it to a quiet room? It doesn't have to be on the same floor.

A: I'll try, Mr. Smith. I'll talk to the receptionist. Well, Mr. Smith, would you move to the adjacent room, that is 518? In the meantime I'll help you with your luggage.

B: Yes, please. And thank you for your patience. You are really very helpful.

A: It's my pleasure. Just try to get hold of me[4] whenever you need my help.

3. A Demanding Tourist 挑剔的游客

(A: Guide; B: Guest)

A: Good morning, Mrs. DuPont. Is everything all right?

B: No, it's not. Someone's stolen some of my valuables——two rings and a gold watch.

A: I'm very sorry to hear that, madam. Where were they?

B: In my room. The door was locked. It can only be one of the staff. I want my things back and fast.

A: Well, I can certainly understand that you're upset about losing them and I'll do all I can to help. If they really are missing, it's a matter for the police.

B: What do you mean, if they are missing? I told you they were.

A: Yes, madam, but first I'll have one of the housekeeping staff look through your room in case they are still there.

B: I do not want anyone from the staff in my room! They are the ones who have taken my belongings so they certainly will not find my jewelry.

A: Now Mrs. DuPont, why do you think the staff robbed you?

B: Well, they are the only people who can enter the rooms freely.

A: Exactly, so don't you think the hotel would be very careful with whom they entrust this freedom? Also, the hotel knows how important it is to protect its reputation if it is to have a successful business. Besides, the staff do not want to lose their jobs and face prosecution. They would be the first to be suspected.

B: Yes, that will do to start. But what if we do not find my things?

A: Then we will tell the duty manager so he can work to see if the hotel can find your belongings. Perhaps you left them somewhere else? If not, I am sure the manager will talk with the housekeeping staff and others who have access to your room. The police will also be notified.

B: That sounds like a good plan.

A: Let's start now, this way. Hopefully we can find your things and you can get back to enjoying your vacation in China!

B: You're right.

4. Complaining about Chamber Service   投诉房间服务

(A: Guide; B: Guest)

B: Sir, I've got something to complain.
A: Yes?
B: I'm afraid the room attendant did not properly clean my room.
A: I'm awfully sorry, Madam. Let me call the housekeeping and have it done right away.
B: There is dust on the chest of drawers⑤.
A: Please let me apologize for this. I'll see to it that a room attendant is to dust it immediately.
B: And there's another problem. The window of my bedroom will not close properly.
A: All right. I'll ask the repairman of the hotel to fix it right away. Are there any other problems, Madam?
B: Yes. I think the linen hasn't been changed for three days.
A: I will talk to the manager of the hotel and make sure that this does not happen again.
B: That's very kind of you.
A: Please do not hesitate to let me know if you have any further problems.
B: Well, I think I've complained enough for today.
A: You are right to complain, Madam. We want to make your stay as comfortable as possible.
B: I must say that everyone has been very nice to me.
A: By the way, both the room attendant and the repairman will be right up⑥.
B: Very well. Thank you very much.
A: You are very welcome, Madam.

Notes   注释

① 行李提取凭证。
② 缺乏人手。
③ don't bother   不用麻烦了。既可用于客气的谢绝，也可用于不客气的拒绝。
④ to get hold of me   来找我；get hold of   有抓住、得到的意思；get hold of the wrong end of the stick   完全误解
⑤ chest of drawers   五斗柜，衣柜
⑥ be right up   马上就到

Useful Sentences   必学句型

1. My luggage seems to be missing.
   我的行李好像不见了。

2. Could I see your luggage claim checks?
   我可以看一下你的行李票吗？

3. Try to get hold of me whenever you need my help.
   需要帮忙的话你可以来找我。

4. Please let me apologize for this.
   请允许我对此向你道歉。

5. Please do not hesitate to contact us again if you have any further problems.
   如还有问题,请立即与我们联系。

6. Let me get a representative from the airline to speak with you.
   让我找航空公司代表来跟你说。

7. What seems to be the problem, Mr. Smith? How can I help you?
   出什么问题了,史密斯先生?我能帮你什么忙吗?

8. I am sorry to hear that. There must have been a mistake.
   很抱歉,肯定是哪里出差错了。

9. This was entirely due to our error. Please accept our sincere apologies for the inconvenience.
   This type of slip-up will never occur on your future tours.
   完全是因为我们的错而给你带来不便,请接受我们真诚的道歉。这种错误在你后面的行程中绝对不会再发生了。

10. There is one more thing.
    还有一件事情。

11. I can certainly understand that you're upset about losing your luggage.
    我完全可以理解你丢失行李的烦恼。

  Passage Reading 阅读材料

A Letter of Complaint

Dear Sir,

  I am writing to you to discuss several incidents that happened to me on my recent tour to China. While I was in China I was very unhappy with the service your staff provided, and found them to be uncaring and very unhelpful towards me and my problems. When I talked to a supervisor in the local office he did not have the time to help me and did not seem interested in finding anyone else to help me. I am writing to you in the hope that other tourists will not go through the same difficulties that I faced and the frustration of having no one listen to me or help me when I needed.

  The first problem I encountered upon entering your country was having most of my luggage lost on the flight between Beijing and Xi'an. I spent three days without a change of clothes and had to buy new ones so that I could go out of the hotel. I was told that everything possible was being done to locate my luggage, but no one could tell me what was being done, or how long it would take. When I did receive my luggage, they wanted me to pay an extra fee for delivering it to the hotel. The tour guide was very unfriendly to me whenever I asked him about my luggage and he was unwilling to help me call the airport to inquire about it.

  The day after I received my luggage, our group ate at a small local restaurant in the middle of the city. Something I ate there made me quite ill that night. I missed the tour the next day and was unable to eat much of anything for the next several days. I feel the guide was very irresponsible taking us into a place that was not clean. I was very upset about this and when I tried to talk to the guide about it he just told me that no one else had ever gotten sick from eating there and that there was nothing to be upset about.

I hope you can realize how much the trip to your country meant to me. I had planned and saved for it for over three years.

The problems I had were common ones to people who travel and not the fault of your company, but I did expect your staff to be more supportive and helpful than they were. At least they could have been a little more understanding of my situation.

Sincerely
Mrs. B. Smith
Boston, Mass.

1. **Reading and Translation**

The Spring Festival

The most important holiday in China is the Spring Festival, also known as the Chinese New Year. To the Chinese people it is as important as Christmas to the West. The date for this annual celebration is determined by the lunar calendar rather than the Gregorian calendar, so the timing of the holiday varies from late January to early February.

Preparations for the New Year begin on the final days of the last lunar month, when most families clean their homes, pay their debts, cut their hair and buy new clothes. Houses are festooned with paper scrolls bearing auspicious poetry. People also burn incense at home and in the temples to pay respect to their ancestors and to pray to the gods for a happy life in the coming months.

On New Year's Eve, all the members of families come together to hold feasts. Jiaozi is popular in the North, while southerners favor a sticky sweet glutinous rice pudding called "Nian'gao". At midnight on New Year's Eve, people set off firecrackers to drive away the evil spirits and to greet the arrival of the New Year. In an instant whole cities are engulfed in the deafening noise of firecrackers.

2. **Complete the Following Dialogues in English with the hints given in Chinese**

（1）（A：Guide；B：Guest）

B：Excuse me. 你是我们的导游吗？

A：Yes, I am. 你是来自美国的史密斯先生吗？

B：Yes. 我们已经在这等了半个多小时了！Why are you so late?

A：I'm terribly sorry. 我们的车子被堵住了。

B：You 应该知道这个时段的交通是很忙的。Why didn't you start earlier?

A：我们确实已比平常提早出发了。But there was an accident which caused a big jam and held us for almost an hour.

B：All right. Now 别让客人们再等了。

A：Right. 我会向客人解释情况的 on the bus.

（2）（A：Guide；B：Manager；C：Guest）

A：先生，这是餐厅的经理。

B：What can I do for you, sir?

C：你是这里的经理吗？我们不得不投诉你们的食物。There was a fly in the fish! Look!

B：Yes, I'm the manager. 真对不起，让你们今晚扫兴了。Please have this croaker instead.

C：但我恐怕我们没点这道菜。

A：我已经跟经理讲好了，There will be no charge for this. 这是他们给你们的补偿。

B：请接受我们的歉意，我保证我们会尽力改善。

C：All right. 我希望今后不要再发生这样的事情。

B：Thank you very much. 我希望你们还会再来我们餐厅 and we'll give you an excellent service as well.

C：Certainly, we will.

B：朋友们，祝你们旅途愉快。

C：Thanks. We will!

3. Role-play

Situation A

It is in mid-October on the day before the West Lake International Firework Festival. Bars have been set up around the lake to protect the viewers. You have an elderly group going to a boat ride on the lake. Seeing the obstacle, the group starts complaining. Discuss among yourselves and see how would you handle this situation.

Situation B

You are taking a big group to visit Lingyin Temple. You told them to follow you closely in case they got lost. But when you come back after visiting the temple, an old couple comes to you angrily to complain that they did not see the temple because they did not follow you for you were walking too fast for them. Try your best to solve this problem.

Part II

OUTBOUND TOURISM
出境旅游

Unit 1

At the Airport (I)
在机场（1）

——Check-in at the Airport
办理登机手续

本课导读

乘机旅行是出境旅游的主要旅行方式。旅行前，领队应向航空公司核对班机时间、旅客人数并确认机位，安排好送客车辆，并在起飞前一小时到达机场。办理登机手续时，应注意班机出发时间与登机时间、通关闸口方向、预定到达时间等。协助游客办理行李托运时，必须清点行李件数，收好登机牌和行李领取证，同时要提醒团员随身携带贵重物品。进入候机室候机时，要注意控制预留时间，一旦通知登机，应立即带领团员按顺序登机。

Special Terms 专业词汇

机场用语			
international airport	国际机场	transfer passenger	中转旅客
domestic airport	国内机场	transfer correspondence	中转处
check-in	（登机手续）办理	way in/entrance	入口
boarding pass (card)	登机牌	exit/out/way out	出口
airport terminal	机场候机楼	goods to declare	报关物品
immigration	护照检查处	nothing to declare	不须报关
arrival	进站（进港、到达）	V.I.P. room	贵宾室
departure	出站（出港、离开）	Custom	海关
passport control	护照检查处	ticket office	购票处
immigration	移民局	cash	付款处
security check	安全检查	gate/boarding gate	登机口
international terminal	国际候机楼	passenger conveyer	自动步行梯
luggage claim/baggage claim	行李领取处	luggage carousel	行李传送带
		departure lounge	候机室
		FLT No. (flight number)	航班号
international departure	国际航班出港	bus/coach service	公共汽车
international passengers	国际航班旅客	taxi	出租车
domestic departure	国内航班出站	taxi pick-up point	出租车乘车点
satellite	卫星楼	coach pick-up point	大轿车乘车点
transfer	中转	airline coach service	航空公司汽车服务处
transit	过境		

Unit 1 At the Airport (I) 在机场 (1)

car hire	租车处（旅客自己驾车）	hand luggage/carry-on luggage	手提行李
arriving from	来自……	checked luggage	过磅行李
scheduled time (SCHED)	预计时间	free luggage allowance	免费托运行李
actual	实际时间		重量
delay	延误	overweight	超重
landed	已降落	charge for overweight luggage	超重费
boarding	登机	personal belonging	随身物品
departure time	起飞时间	luggage claim	行李领取处
public phone	公用电话		
toilet/lavatory/rest room	厕所	**机票用语**	
men's/gent's/gentlemen's	男厕	endorsement/restrictions	(指限定条件)
women's/lady's	女厕	to…	前往……
restaurant	餐厅	from…	从……
greeting arriving	迎宾处	name of passenger	旅客姓名
bar	酒吧	carrier	承运人（公司）
coffee shop/cafe	咖啡馆	good for passage between	旅行经停地点
departure to	前往……	flight No.	航班号
stairs and lifts to departures	由此乘电梯前往登机	seat No.	机座号
		plane No.	机号
up/upstairs	由此上楼	class (fare basis)	(座舱) 等级
down/downstairs	由此下楼	first class	头等舱
duty-free shop	免税店	business class	公务舱
bank	银行	economy class	经济舱
post office	邮局	date	起飞日期
currency exchange	货币兑换处	time	起飞时间
rail ticket	出售火车票	status	订座情况
hotel reservation	订旅馆	smoking seat	吸烟座位
tour arrangement	旅行安排	non-smoking seat	非吸烟席
luggage locker	行李暂存箱	ticket confirm	机票确认
luggage tag	行李牌	boarding gate	登机口

Situational Conversations 情景对话

1. At the Information Desk 在问询处

(A: Clerk of the Airline; B: Tour Leader)

Scene 1

A: Good morning. Can I help you?

B: Yes, I'd like to know whether there is a flight to Frankfurt.

A: Yes, there is. Flight 217 departs at 10:30 a.m. and arrives in Frankfurt at 12:30 a.m..

B: How many flights do you have to Frankfurt every week?

A: Three flights, on Sunday, Tuesday and Friday.

B: OK. Thanks a lot.

Scene 2

B: Excuse me. We have a connecting flight on MH 235 to Kuala Lumpur①. Where do we check in our luggage?

A: Please go to the counter beside the information desk.

B: When will the flight begin boarding?

A: The flight will begin boarding around 14:20. Please wait at the waiting room until it's announced.

B: I see. Thank you.

Scene 3

A: Good afternoon, madam. May I help you?

B: Could you tell me where I check in for the flight NH203 to Tokyo②?

A: Down to the far end of the lounge and you'll find the counter for flights to Tokyo.

B: Do you know when they begin to check in?

A: What is the departure time of your flight?

B: 1:30 p.m.

A: Let me see. It's 11:00 a.m. now. So they will start in about an hour.

B: Thank you very much. By the way, where can I make a phone call?

A: You'll find phone booths upstairs, madam.

B: Thanks.

A: It's my pleasure.

2. At the Check-in Counter 换登机牌

(A: Clerk of the Check-in Counter; B: Tour Leader)

Scene 1

A: Good morning, sir. What can I do for you?

B: Is this the counter for SQ 368 to Singapore③?

A: Yes, sir. Are you from the same group?

B: Yes. We are.

A: Please go to the next counter for group check-in.

* * *

B: Hello, we are a group of 30 people going to Melbourne by QF 238④.

A: May I have your tickets and passports, please?

B: Sure, here you are.

A: How many pieces of luggage would you like to check in?

B: Thirty five pieces altogether.

A: Here are your tickets, passports and boarding passes. Your luggage claim tags are attached to the tickets cover.

B: Thank you.

A: You're welcome.

Scene 2

A: Good evening, ma'am. May I help you?

B: Yes. I'd like to check in, please.

A: May I see your ticket and passport, please?

B: Here you are.

A: Do you have any luggage to check?

B: No, I've this traveling only.

A: I see. Here are your ticket and boarding pass, ma'am. Your seat is 3-C. It's an aisle seat. And your flight will be called within about 10 minutes.

B: Thanks a lot.

3. Luggage Check-in 行李托运

(A: Clerk of the Check-in Counter; B: Tour Leader)

Scene 1

B: Excuse me, miss, Should I check in here for taking flight AF310 to Paris[5]?

A: Yes, sir. May I have your passport and flight ticket, please?

B: Sure, here are ten tickets and passports. We are from the same tour group. Can we have six window seats and four aisle seats?

A: Let me see…OK. No problem. Do you have any pieces of luggage to check in?

B: Yes. We have eight suitcases and two bags.

A: Would you please put them on the scale?

B: Of course. They are not overweight, are they?

A: I'm sorry. They are 5 kilograms over.

B: That's too bad. It must be because of the brochures.

A: I see you don't have any carry-on luggage. Probably, you could pick some brochures out of your luggage and take them with you.

B: Good idea. Could you explain the free baggage allowance to me?

A: Of course. On trans-continental flights to France, your free baggage allowance is not more than 30 kilograms each.

B: I see.

A: All right. Here are your baggage claim tags, flight tickets, boarding passes and passports.

B: When is the boarding time?

A: The boarding time is 8:45 p.m. and you will board from Gate 18.

B: How do I find Gate 18 from here?

A: Take the escalator over there and turn left. You'll see the sign.

B: Thank you very much.

Scene 2

A: May I help you, sir?

B: Yes, We're here to check in for the flight to Sydney. Here are our tickets and passports.

A: Thank you, sir. Please put your baggage on the scale. How many pieces of baggage do you want to check?

B: Twenty pieces altogether. Can I take this traveling bag as a carry-on?

A: I'm afraid not. It's overweight. The allowance for the carry-on baggage is 8 kg.

B: I see.

A: Here are twenty claim tags for your baggage and your passports.

B: Thank you very much.

4. Transit and Transfer[6]　过境与转机

(A: Clerk of the Airline; B: Tour Leader)

Scene 1

A: Good afternoon. May I help you?

B: Yes, we are to transfer to flight NH 588 to Tokyo. We'd like to check in now.

A: May I have your tickets and passports, please?

B: Certainly, here are ten tickets. Can we have our seats close to each other?

A: Let me see. The airplane is quite full now. I can hardly give you ten seats together. But I'll try to make it for you.

B: Thank you, sir.

A: Here are your tickets, passports and boarding passes. I have arranged your seats as close to each other as possible. The departure time for the flight is 11:15 a.m. Please board at Gate 28.

B: Could you tell me the way to the boarding gate?

A: Certainly, sir. Just take the escalator down to the nest floor, get on the passenger's conveyer to the area, and you'll easily find Gate 28 there. You may wait in the departure lounge for boarding since there is not much time left.

B: I see. Thank you very much for your help.

A: It's my pleasure.

Scene 2

A: What can I do for you, ma'am?

B: I thought what I took was a "non-stop flight". Why do I have to transit here?

A: I am sorry, ma'am. Your ticket shows that your flight will fly directly to Paris. You don't have to change flights, but you do have to stop over here for about two hours.

B: I am a little confused. Do you mean "non-stop flight" and "direct flight" are not the same?

A: No, they are not. Non-stop flight won't make any stops during the flight.

B: What about direct flights?

A: Direct flights just mean you don't have to make any connection on the way to the destination.

B: Oh. Now I see. Well, if I had to transfer here and continue my journey to Vienna, what should I do?

A: Then, you would have to go to the Transfer Counter and recheck in.

B: Will I get a new boarding pass?

A: Yes, you will.

B: Thank you for your detailed explanation. Now, how long should I wait here?

A: About two hours.

B: Since there are still two hours to wait, could you show me some place to have a drink?

A: Sure. Do you see the sign over here?

B: Yes. The yellow one?

A: Right. Just go straight and then turn right. You will see a coffee shop right on your left hand side.

B: I see. What time do we board again?

A: Your flight will depart at 4:00 p.m. However, you might need to get ready for boarding 40 minutes before the departure.

B: All right. Thanks a lot for your help.

5. Getting Aboard a Flight 登机

(A: Stewardess; B: Tourist)

Scene 1

A: Good morning. Welcome aboard. This way, please.

B: Thank you, stewardess. Can you direct me to my seat?

A: Certainly, may I see your boarding pass, please?

B: Sure, here it is.

A: It's 32-B. Just over there, sir.

B: Thank you, miss. Where can I put my bag?

A: You can put your coat and small things on the tack over your head and your bag here at your feet.

B: Can I put my bag in this empty seat beside me?

A: I'm sorry. All carry-on luggages must be placed underneath the seat in front of you or in the overhead compartment.

B: Where is the button that controls my chair?

A: Right here on the arm rest.

B: Thank you.

Scene 2

B: Excuse me, miss. My wife and I were assigned separate seats. Do you have any empty seats together somewhere?

A: Would you wait a moment, please? I'll check for you.

B: Thank you, miss.

(A few minutes later)

A: Sir, we have some seats available in the back of the cabin. Would that be all right?

B: Yes, thank you very much. May I use the lavatory now?

A: Would you wait until after we take off? We'll be leaving very shortly.

6. Airport Announcements　机场广播

(A: Announcer; B: Tourist; C: Passenger Service Agent)

Scene 1

A: Qantas Airways announces the departure of Flight 810 to Melbourne. Will passengers for this flight please go to Gate 7?

B: Excuse me, sir. Did they say Melbourne?

C: Yes, Flight 810 to Melbourne.

B: Where should we board the plane?

C: Please go to Gate 7.

B: Thank you for your help, sir.

Scene 2

A: Air France regrets to announce that Flight 808 to Geneva, scheduled to depart at 2:00 p.m. has been delayed on account of big fog. This flight will depart at 2:40 p.m.. Passengers with connecting flights will be met by an Air France ticket agent on arrival in Genevese.

B: Excuse me, miss. Which flight is delayed?

C: The flight to Geneva.

B: For how long?

C: 40 minutes.

Scene 3

A: This is the final call for TG flight 260 to Bangkok[⑦], now boarding at Gate 15. Please have your boarding pass ready.

B: Final call for Bangkok?

C: Sure.

B: But where is Gate 15?

C: Follow me, please.

Notes　注释

① We have a connecting flight on MH 235 to Kuala Lumpur.　我们要转乘马航235次航班去吉隆坡。

connecting flight　转接航班; MH: Malaysia Airlines　马来西亚航空公司; Kuala Lumpur　吉隆坡, 马来西亚的首都

② ...check in for the flight NH203 to Tokyo.　办理全日空前往东京的203次航班的登机手续。

NH: All Nippon Airways Co Ltd.　全日空航空公司

③ SQ 368 to Singapore 新加坡航空公司前往新加坡的 368 次航班。
SQ：Singapore Airlines 新加坡航空公司
④ going to Melbourne by QF 238 乘坐澳洲航空公司的 238 次航班去墨尔本。
QF：Qantas Airways Ltd. 澳洲航空公司
⑤ Should I check in here for taking flight AF310 to Paris? 乘坐法航前往巴黎的 310 次航班是在这儿办理登机手续吗？
AF：Air France 法国航空公司
⑥ transit and transfer 过境与转机
过境是指旅客因所搭乘的班机在途中补充油料，更换机组人员而在机场做短暂停留，通常不须换飞机；转机指旅客所乘的不是直飞班机（direct flight），而必须在途中某机场转乘另一架飞机到达。
⑦ This is the final call for TG flight 260 to Bangkok. 这是对泰航前往曼谷的 260 次航班的最后一次通报。
TG：Thai Airways International Ltd. 泰国国际航空公司
Bangkok 曼谷，泰国首都

Useful Sentences 必学句型

1. Is this the right counter to check in for the flight to Sydney?
   这是到悉尼去的航班登记处吗？
2. Can I have my luggage checked here for the flight to Bangkok?
   请问我能在这里办理到曼谷航班的行李托运手续吗？
3. Where can I get my boarding pass and have my luggage weighed?
   请问在哪里换登机牌，给行李称重？
4. What are the check-in procedures?
   登机手续有哪些？
5. Is the plane on schedule?
   飞机会准时起飞吗？
6. What's the departure time of the flight?
   飞机什么时候起飞？
7. Please wait at the departure lounge until it's announced.
   请到候机室等待通知。
8. How many pieces of checked luggage have you got?
   你有多少行李要托运？
9. You have to X-ray your bag for a label.
   你的箱子需要经过 X 光检查，贴上验放标签。
10. Can I take this as a carry-on?
    我可以随身携带这东西吗？
11. Here are two tags for the suitcases and two labels for the hand luggage.
    这是行李箱的两张标签，这是手提行李的两张标签。

12. Your luggage exceeds the free baggage allowance.
    您的行李超过免费限额。
13. What's the luggage allowance, please?
    请问免费行李有什么规定?
14. 30 kilograms free luggage allowance for first class and 20 kilograms for economy class.
    头等舱允许携带 30 千克免费行李，经济舱允许携带 20 千克免费行李。
15. Do you have any seat preferences?
    您对座位有什么偏好吗?
16. Which seat do you prefer, a window seat or an aisle seat?
    您喜欢什么样的座位，是靠窗的，还是靠通道的?
17. Can I have a seat in the back of the plane?
    可以给我一个靠近机尾的座位吗?
18. You will have to show the boarding pass on your way to board the plane.
    上机时，你得出示登机牌。
19. Please don't forget to claim your checked luggage.
    请记住领取您的托运行李。
20. You may carry one piece of hand luggage into cabin.
    您可以随身带一件手提行李上机。
21. Let me take some stuff out as hand luggage. Is that all right?
    我可以拿一些东西出来当手提行李吗?
22. Where should I take my connecting flight?
    我该在哪里搭乘接驳的班机?
23. Can I make a connecting flight here to LA?
    我可以在这里转机到洛杉矶吗?
24. How long do we have to wait here?
    我们必须在这里等多久?
25. I lost my transit card. What should I do now?
    我的过境证丢了，怎么办?
26. How do I get to the transit lounge from here?
    从这里要怎么找到过境室?
27. This bag is for storage in an overhead bin or under the seat.
    这件行李可放在头顶上方的行李箱里或放在座位底下。
28. Thai Airways announces the departure of Flight 454 to Bangkok. Will passengers for this flight please go to Gate 7.
    泰国航空公司飞往曼谷的 454 次航班就要起飞了，请乘坐这次航班的旅客到 7 号门登机。
29. Passengers from Shanghai. You have arrived at Australia's capital, Canberra. Please proceed to the luggage claim area to get your luggage.
    从上海来的旅客们请注意，你们已经到达澳大利亚首都堪培拉，请去行李房取行李。

30. Your attention, please. Flight BA 328 from London will be one hour late on account of big fog.

旅客们请注意，由伦敦飞来的英航328次班机因为大雾天气，将要晚点一小时到达。

 Passage Reading   阅读材料

The Passenger Terminal

Passengers begin and end their flights at the passenger terminal. Airports may have one or more terminal buildings. At the various airlines' ticket counters, departing passengers purchase tickets or have their tickets checked. They also have their baggage checked. Loudspeakers, television screens, and lighted boards announce flight arrivals and departures. Boarding lounges provide seats for travelers and their friends. Passengers board and leave aircraft from terminal locations called gates. At most large airports, a covered walkway called a boarding bridge connects the gate with the aircraft during boarding. Arriving passengers pick up their luggage at a baggage claim area in the passenger terminal.

Many of the activities in the passenger terminal go on behind the scenes. Most large air carrier airports are operating with the help of weather service stations, which gives airlines and other operators of aircraft general information on weather conditions throughout the country as well as around the world. Most airlines also have their own weather services to check conditions for specific flights.

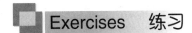 Exercises   练习

1. Reading and Translation

Statue of Liberty

The statue of liberty is a huge statue in the New York Harbor. It is a gift presented to America by France to commemorate (纪念) the birth of the United States and the continuing friendship between the French and American people.

The cost of the statue itself, about $250 000, was raised in France, while the funds for the pedestal (底座), about $350 000, were raised in the United States.

The statue itself—the figure of a woman—weighs 225 tons and its height is 46 meters, with the pedestal, 93 meters. The woman figure holds a torch (火炬) in her right hand and in her left arm she carries a book which means the U.S. Declaration of the Independence. Each of the figure's eyes is 0.79 meter wide and 40 people can stand inside her head. The observation platform (瞭望台) in the figure's head is 79 meters above the sea level and offers a splendid view of the New York Harbor, especially at night when the torch gives orange color light.

The huge statue at the entrance of New York harbor is welcoming the peoples of the world with the torch of liberty.

2. Complete the Following Dialogues in English with the hints given in Chinese

（1）（A：Clerk；B：Tourist）

A：下午好，请出示您的机票和护照。

B：_____

A：谢谢，您有行李吗？

B：_____

A：您是要靠窗的座位还是靠过道的座位？

B：_____

A：这是您的行李票和登机牌。

（2）（A：Stewardess；B：Tourist）

A：早晨好，欢迎乘坐本次航班。

B：_____

A：当然能，我可以看看您的登机牌吗？

B：_____

3. Role-play

Situation A

You are a tour leader. You have 20 members in your tour group. You are going to Tokyo by Flight NH 108. You have got 24 pieces of luggage all together. You check in for your group at the check-in counter of All Nippon Airways. Ask the clerk to help you.

Situation B

You are a tour leader. You are taking a group to transfer to Flight OZ 312 to Seoul. Your plane leaves at Gate 8 but you take the group to Gate 18. You ask an airport clerk to help you. Make up a dialogue between the clerk and you.

Unit 2 At the Airport (Ⅱ) 在机场（2）

—— Going through Immigration and Customs 办理出入境手续

本课导读

领队在出境前，应先将出入境的程序简略介绍给游客，并帮助游客填好出入境卡。当领队办理有关手续时，可选择一名游客负责把其他客人集合在一起。办理出入境手续时，要看清自己排的队是在"本国人"还是在"外国人"窗口，以免浪费时间。接受检查时，将团队名单及护照交移民官检查，并让游客按名单上的顺序排好队，依次通过。办完入境证照检验后领取行李时，领队要确认自己班机的行李在第几号行李转盘上出现。万一有行李遗失，则必须立刻通知航空公司地勤人员，尽快办理遗失行李的登记手续。过海关前，领队须帮助游客如实填好关税申报表；通关时，将需要海关申报的游客的护照分出，让其持护照和机票走红色通道。

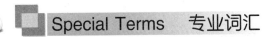

Special Terms 专业词汇

出（入）境用语			
arrival card	入境卡	worker	工人
departure card	出境卡	farmer	农民
family name	姓	commerce (business people)	商业人员
first (given) name	名	jobless	无业
year	年	others	其他
month	月	country of origin	原住地
day	日	service agent	服务人员
sex	性别	destination country	前往目的地国
male	男	city where you boarded	登机城市
female	女	address while in	前往国家的住址
date of birth (birth date)	出生日期	number and street	街道及门牌号
accompanying number	偕行人数	city and state	城市及国家
occupation	职业	signature	签名
professionals & technical	专业技术人员	official use only	官方填写
nationality/country of citizenship		city where visa was issued	签证签发地
	国籍	date of issue	签发日期
clerk	办事员	customs declaration	海关申报
		goods to declare	申报物品

customs inspector	海关检查员	back bag	背包
port of entry	入境城市	deliver	运送
customs duty	海关税		
immunization	免疫	**签证用语**	
vaccination certificate	防疫证书	visa	签证
Health Certificate for International Travelers		group visa	团体签证
	国际旅行健康证明书	visa type	签证种类
quarantine formalities	检疫手续	expiry date（或 before）	失效日期（或必须在……日之前入境）
baggage claim area	行李提取区		
baggage service	行李服务处	for stays of	停留期为……
cart	推车	nationality	国籍
hand truck	手推车	Passport No.	护照号
misplace	错放	control No.	编号
damage	损坏	Issue At	签发地
compensate	补偿	Issue Date（或 On）	签发日期
compensation	补偿		

 Situational Conversations   情景对话

1. Going Through the Security Check   行李安检

（A：Security Inspector；B：Tourist）

Scene 1

A：Good morning, sir. Do you have any unexposed films in this bag?

B：No. I haven't.

A：Will you please put your bag on the conveyer belt?

B：Sure.

A：Would you please put your watch, keys and other metal articles into this tray? Now, please walk through the gate and collect your bag and other personal belongings at the other side.

B：I see. Thank you.

Scene 2

A：Good evening, madam. Could you put that bag on the counter and open it, please? What is inside?

B：Some clothes, my shaving kit, a couple of books and some souvenirs①.

A：Do you have anything else?

B：Let me see. Oh, yes, a pack of green tea and some bananas.

A：I'm sorry, sir. You are not supposed to bring fresh fruits into Germany. I'm going to confiscate them.

B：Oh, that's too bad.

A: Can I leave now?

A: Well, you are in the clear now. Sorry to have bothered you.

B: That's all right.

2. Going Through the Immigration Formalities 办理入境手续

(A: Immigration Official; B: Tour Leader)

Scene 1

A: Good morning. Please show your ticket, passport and immigration card.

B: Here you are.

A: What's the purpose of your visit in this country? On business or for pleasure[②]?

B: On business. I'm here with a tour group.

A: So you are a tour leader, aren't you?

B: Yes. We have several places to visit.

A: How long will you be staying in New Zealand?

B: 5 days. We'll be leaving on May 25th.

A: Where do you intend to stay while in the country?

B: In the hotels.

A: How much currencies have you got?

B: I have 2 000 US dollars in cash.

A: Do you have a return ticket?

B: Yes, here you are. Can I leave now?

A: Just a second. Do you remember when you got your last vaccination?

B: Three days ago, just before I came here. You may check my health certification.

A: OK. I think you are cleared. Thank you for your cooperation.

Scene 2

A: Good afternoon, sir. May I have your passport and arrival card, please[③]?

B: I'm the leader of a tour group. We have a group visa.

A: Please show it and all the members' passports to me.

B: Certainly, sir. Here you are.

A: Leader, why is this passenger's date of birth is different from that in his passport?

B: Let me have a look. Oh, I had made a mistake when I filled in the visa form. Sorry, would you please correct it for me?

A: Sure. Please let me have the address, telephone number and name of the linkman of the local travel agency[④].

B: No problem.

A: Please let your passengers keep their arrival cards in their passports, and go through one by one according to the order of the name list[⑤].

B: Yes. Can I be the last one to pass, sir?

A: Sure, you can.

3. Claiming the Luggage 提取行李

Scene 1

(A: Clerk of the Airport; B: Passenger)

A: Good morning, sir. May I help you?

B: Yes. I came from Hangzhou by CA 558⑥. Where can I get my luggage?

A: The luggage claim area is downstairs.

B: Which carousel is for the luggage from Hangzhou?

A: The one on the left, No. 2.

* * *

B: Excuse me, sir. I can't find my baggage. Here is my claim tag.

A: Don't worry, sir. Can you describe your baggage?

B: One is medium-sized Polo, and it's gray. The other is a large leather suitcase with my name tag. It's dark blue.

A: Are those yours, sir? I'm afraid you've come to the wrong place.

B: Oh, they are mine. Thank you very much. But the handle of my suitcase is broken. Where can I go to report it?

B: Please go to the Luggage Service over there. The clerks there will help you.

A: I see.

Scene 2

(A: Clerk of the Luggage Service; B: Tourist)

A: Is this where I go about lost baggage?

B: Yes, sir. May I help you?

A: Well, one of my suitcases hasn't shown up.

B: What flight were you on?

A: Thai Airway, Flight 236.

B: And what does the suitcase look like?

A: It's a gray leather suitcase.

B: OK. Can I see your baggage claim check?

A: Here it is.

B: All right, sir. Why don't you have a look over there on those shelves? That's the unclaimed baggage from Thai Airways flights today.

(A few minutes later)

B: Have you got it?

A: Yes. You know, I really need this suitcase. All my clothes are in the suitcase. Thank you very much indeed.

B: It's our pleasure to serve you.

Scene 3

A: What can I do for you?

B: I've been waiting in the baggage claim area for one hour, but still can't find my luggage.

Unit 2　At the Airport (II)　在机场 (2)

A: What kind of luggage?

B: One big blue suitcase and one red backpack.

A: May I know your airline company and the flight number?

B: It's Japan Airlines. The flight number is 516.

A: Do you have the baggage claim tags?

B: Here you are.

A: I'm sorry. Your luggage was probably misplaced in Tokyo while you transited there.

B: What should I do now?

A: Would you please fill out this form and leave your address and phone number where we can contact you?

B: When can I get the information?

A: About 10 o'clock tonight. Once we find your luggage, we'll contact you as soon as possible⑦.

B: Do I have to come here again?

A: No. We'll deliver them to where you are staying.

B: OK. I'll be in the hotel downtown for two days. But what if my luggage was damaged?

A: Then, we will give you reasonable compensation for it.

B: So that's it?

A: Yes, that's it. Again, we are terribly sorry for the inconvenience.

4. Customs Clearance　通关

(A: Customs Inspector; B: Passenger)

Scene 1

A: Please show me your customs declaration form, sir.

B: Certainly. Here it is.

A: Do you have anything to declare?

B: No, I don't.

A: Please open this bag. What are these?

B: These are for my personal use. And these are gifts for my friends.

A: Do you have any liquor or cigarettes?

B: Yes, I have five bottles of brandy.

A: You'll have to pay duty on that. Do you have any other baggage?

B: No.

A: OK. Please give this declaration form to that official at the exit.

Scene 2

(A: Customs Inspector; B: Passenger)

A: Anything to declare?

B: I suppose no, except a carton of cigarettes⑧. That's duty-free, isn't it?

A: Yes, one can bring in one carton duty-free. Will you open your suitcase, please?

B: Certainly. Only personal effects.

A: Is that a new camera?

B: No, it's an old one.

A: May I see it, please?

B: Of course.

A: When did you buy it?

B: Last year. I've a receipt of it.

A: All right. You may go through now.

Scene 3

A: May I see your ticket, passport and exit card, please?

B: Here you are.

A: Do you have your customs declaration?

B: May I give an oral declaration?

A: All right. What do you declare?

B: I've brought along three iPads^⑨. They are gifts for my friends.

A: Get them out and let me have a look, will you?

B: Certainly, here you are.

A: They are dutiable. The rate is 25%。

B: I see.

A: Have you got the invoice with you?

B: Yes. Here you are, officer.

5. Going Through the Emigration Formalities 办理出境手续

Scene 1

　　(A: Immigration Officer; B: Tourist; C: Customs Inspector)

A: May I have your passport and exit card, please?

B: Certainly, officer, here you are.

A: It's all right. Please go to the Customs.

C: Please show your Customs Declaration, sir. Do you have anything do declare?

B: No, I don't think so.

A: Well, would you mind opening this bag?

B: I guess not.

A: Let me examine your luggage and check it with your declaration form.

A: Please show me the valuable articles you brought in.

B: Certainly, officer.

A: Do you still have this article?

B: I'm sorry. It has lost.

A: Do you have a certificate for the loss?

B: Yes. This is the certificate for the loss.

A: All right. Everything is fine. Your luggage is passed.

Scene 2

(A: Customs Inspector; B: Tourist)

A: May I have your Declaration Form?

B: Certainly, sir. Here you are.

A: All right. Do you have anything special to declare?

B: No, I don't think so. I bought a bottle of XO at the duty-free shop⑩, but that's for my personal use.

A: I see. Could you put the suitcase on the counter? I have to take a look at it.

B: Certainly. I'll open it right now.

A: What's this? It does not look like tonic.

B: No. It's medicine for my stomach. Here is the prescription from my doctor.

A: OK. How about this box? It looks like a music player.

B: Yes. There is an iPad 2 for my daughter.

A: Do you know its value?

B: About 450 dollars, I guess. Here is the receipt.

A: That will be fine, then. What about these chocolate candies?

B: They are gifts for my friends. Do I have to pay duty on them?

A: No, since they are not expensive, you don't have to pay.

B: So, can I leave now?

A: Yes. I think you are cleared. Next one, please.

Notes 注释

① Some clothes, my shaving kit, a couple of books and some souvenirs.   有一些衣服、刮胡工具、几本书和一些纪念品。
   kit   成套用具, 用具包。比如, sewing kit   针线包, first aid kit   急救药箱, travel kit   旅行用品
   a couple of   几个, 三两个; in a couple of days   过三两天后

② On business or for pleasure? Are you here on business or for pleasure?   你是来做生意还是来观光的?

③ May I have your passport and arrival card, please?   请出示您的护照和入境卡。
   arrival card 或 entry card 或 disembarkation card 或 incoming passenger card   入境卡;
   departure card 或 exit card 或 embarkation card 或 outgoing passenger card   出境卡

④ the linkman of the local travel agency   当地旅行社的联系人
   linkman 联系人; local travel agency 当地旅行社

⑤ …go through one by one according to the order of the name list.   按照名单上的顺序, 依次通过。
   one by one   一个一个地, 依次地; solve the problems one by one   一个一个地解决问题;
   according to   根据, 按照, 按照……所说, 取决于; according to today's paper   根据今天的所载

⑥ I came from Hangzhou by CA 558.　我乘国航 558 次航班从杭州来。
　　CA：Air China　中国国际航空股份有限公司

⑦ We'll contact you as soon as possible.　我们将尽快和您联系。
　　as soon as possible　尽快地，马上；as…as possible　尽可能

⑧ I suppose no, except a carton of cigarettes.　除了一条香烟外，我想没有其他东西。
　　suppose　料想，认为，以为；a carton of　一条，一纸盒（箱）的量

⑨ I've brought along three iPads.　我带了三台苹果平板电脑。
　　bring along　随身带着；iPad　苹果平板电脑

⑩ I bought a bottle of XO at the duty-free shop.　我在免税商店买了一瓶 XO。
　　XO　特级白兰地；50 年陈年白兰地

Useful Sentences　必学句型

1. What's the purpose of your visit here?
   你此行的目的是什么？

2. I'm traveling with a tourist group. I'm the tour leader of the group.
   我随团旅行。我是该团的领队。

3. I am just passing through the country.
   我只是路过贵国。

4. How long do you intend to stay in the country?
   您打算在此地停留多久？

5. Where are you going to stay in LA?
   您会住在洛杉矶什么地方？

6. How much money are you carrying?
   您带了多少现金？

7. I have 5000 US dollars in cash.
   我带了五千美元现金。

8. You have declared less US dollars.
   您申报的美元数额比随身带的少。

9. Are you going to visit any other places?
   你们还要去其他地方游玩吗？

10. What are you going to do while you are here?
    在此地期间，你打算做些什么？

11. What do I have to do if I need to stay longer?
    如果要停留久一点，我该办理什么手续？

12. This is your passport. You may go to the baggage claim area and get your luggage, then proceed through the customs.
    这是您的护照，您可以到行李提取处取您的行李，然后进行海关检查。

13. I've got my Health Certificate for International Travelers.
    我随身带了国际旅行健康证明书。

14. May I have your Health Certificate and Vaccination Certificate?
    请把你的健康证明书和防疫证明给我?

15. Could I see your passport for cross-checking?
    我能核对一下您的护照吗?

16. I'm from the Quarantine Authority.
    我是卫生防疫部门的官员。

17. Would you show me the baggage claim area for SQ Flight 318?
    请问新航318次班机的行李提取处在哪里?

18. Has all of the luggage come out already?
    所有的行李都出来了吗?

19. Which belt is for the baggage from Flight OZ118?
    哪条传送带传的是韩亚航空118次班机的行李?

20. Please check your luggage claim tags.
    请核对一下行李领取证。

21. One of my bags is missing.
    我掉了一件行李。

22. My suitcase hasn't arrived yet.
    我的手提箱还没有到。

23. I'd like to know when my luggage will arrive.
    我想知道我的行李何时会到。

24. What does your bags look like?
    你的行李是什么样子?

25. I would like to be compensated for the damage to my luggage.
    我想要行李损坏赔偿。

26. Will the airline pay for the damage?
    航空公司会赔偿吗?

27. Please send my baggage to me as soon as possible.
    请尽快将行李送来给我。

28. Do I have to come here for my suitcase?
    我必须要回到这里拿我的手提箱吗?

29. Anything special to declare?
    是否有特别的东西要申报?

30. I have nothing to declare.
    我没有什么要申报。

31. Do you carry any spirits and tobacco?
    有没有带烈性酒和香烟?

32. What's the value of this camera?
    这部相机价值多少?

33. We have to look through everything.
    我们必须一一检查。

34. I am not carrying any foreign currency with me.
    我没有携带任何外币。

35. These are all my personal items.
    这些全是我的个人用品。

36. Everything in the suitcase is for my personal use.
    箱子里的每样东西都是我个人要用的。

37. Do I have to pay tax on this?
    我必须为此付税吗?

38. Let me examine your luggage and check it with your form.
    让我按申报单检查一下你的东西。

39. I have something to declare. Here is my declaration.
    我有东西要申报。这是我的关税申报单。

40. These are personal daily necessities.
    这些是个人的日常用品（盥洗用品）。

41. I haven't got any dutiable things with me.
    我没带应交税的东西。

42. I've only brought some personal things and a few small gifts for friends.
    我只带了些个人用品及给朋友捎带的小礼物。

43. You can go through the green channel.
    你可以走绿色通道。

44. Go through the red channel if you have something to declare.
    若有物品要申报可以走红色通道。

45. Your luggage is passed.
    你的行李已经放行。

  Passage Reading 阅读材料

Immigration and Emigration

Immigration means entering a country to live there. Emigration means leaving one's country to live somewhere else. Many countries call the cards that they ask arriving travelers to fill out "immigration cards" regardless of whether the travelers intend to stay and live in the country or are tourists on a visit. These cards may also be called "arrival" or "disembarkation" cards. Disembark means to leave ship or an aircraft. Some countries also have special "departure" or "embarkation" cards that they ask people to fill out when they leave the country.

The immigration cards ask for information about the passengers. The tourism department uses this information in planning facilities for tourists.

The immigration cards filled out by the passengers help the tourism department know what kinds of travelers visit a country. Answers to questions on the cards give the country of origin, which is the place the tourist comes from, and other important information. This information helps the tourism department know in which countries they should advertise.

The other card the passengers are requested to fill out is a customs declaration. This is a statement that travelers make about the things they are bringing into a country. Most countries tax the items that their citizens purchased in other countries to bring back home. This tax is called a duty. It does not usually apply to tourists visiting a country. However, customs officials want to be sure that tourists are not bringing in things that are against the law or things to sell to people who live outside the country. So every entering traveler fills out customs declaration card in addition to the immigration card.

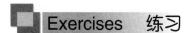

Exercises 练习

1. Reading and Translation

Passport

A passport is a travel document that identifies the holder as a citizen of the country. A passport also requests other countries to give the holder safe passage and all lawful aid and protection. Sometimes a passport must have a visa (official endorsement) from the country a person desires to visit before entry into that country is permitted.

Generally, the government issues three types of passports: (1) diplomatic, for people going abroad on important government assignments; (2) official, for other government employees; (3) regular, for people traveling oversees for personal reason.

Many countries do not require citizens of certain other countries to have passports. Malaysian citizens, for instance, do not need passports to enter Singapore.

Visa

A visa is an endorsement that government officials place on a passport to show that the passport is valid. Officials of the country a traveler is entering grant the visa. The visa certifies that the traveler's passport has been examined and approved. Immigration officials then permit the bearer to enter the country. A government that does not want a person to enter the country can refuse to grant that person a visa.

2. Complete the Following Dialogues in English with the hints given in Chinese

(1) (A: Immigration Official; B: Tour Leader)

A: 你入境的目的是什么?
B: _____
A: 你从事什么职业?
B: _____
A: 你准备在这个国家逗留多长时间?
B: _____
A: 你随身带了多少外币?
B: _____
A: 你的一切手续齐备。祝你在此过得愉快。
B: _____

（2）（A：Customs Official；B：Tourist）

A：有什么要申报吗？

B：_____

A：对，一个人可以带入两瓶免税的酒。请打开手提箱好吗？

B：_____

A：这是一台新的照相机吗？

B：_____

A：我可以看一下吗？

B：_____

3. **Role-play**

Situation A

Your group has just arrived in Bangkok by air. You have to go through Customs after landing. You have got bottles of alcohol for your own use. Make up a dialogue between you and a Customs official.

Situation B

You are traveling with a group as a tour leader. You are going for immigration. There are 25 tourists in your group. Make up a dialogue between an immigration official and you.

Unit 3 On the Airliner 在飞机上

本课导读

乘坐飞机时，为避免遗失，全团机票由领队统一保管。分配座位时，一般按客人名单顺序或通过事先抽签的方式决定座次。由于语言受限，乘坐外国航班时，许多游客往往不敢开口要求机上服务。领队应能清楚地帮助团友表达所需，训练有素的机上乘务员大都可以应客人的要求提供周到的服务，从供应饮食、安排娱乐活动到提供空中购物以及救助伤病不适的旅客。维护本团游客享受服务的权益，是领队的职责。

Special Terms 专业词汇

plane, aircraft	飞机	outside air temperature	外面的气温
jet aircraft	喷气客机	turbulence	乱流
pilot	驾驶员	life vest under your seat	救生圈在座椅下
captain	机长	fasten seat belt while seated	
air crew	机组人员		坐下后系好安全带
steward	男乘务员	safety on board	乘机安全
stewardess	女乘务员	lavatories in rear	盥洗室在后部
ground crew	地勤人员	in-flight	飞行中
cabin	机舱	cloudy	有云的
air sick	晕机	foggy	有雾的
sickness bag	机上清洁袋，呕吐袋	transit stop	过境停留
emergency exit	紧急出口	oxygen mask	氧气罩
occupied	（厕所）有人	life jacket	救生衣
vacant	（厕所）无人	in-flight magazine	机上杂志
in-flight service	空中服务	reading lamp	阅读灯
overhead bin/overhead compartment		first class passenger	头等舱旅客
	头顶上方的行李柜	economy passenger	普通舱旅客
overhead light	顶灯	at the altitude of	高度
arrival time	抵达时间	at the speed of	速度
departure time	起飞时间	blanket	毛毯
local time at origin	出发地的当地时间	pillow	枕头
time to destination	到目的地时间	first-aid-kit	急救包
distance to destination	到目的地距离	light meal	便餐

snack	点心	Pepsi	百事可乐
instant noodle	泡面	Seven-up	七喜汽水
cream	奶油	mineral water	矿泉水
sugar	糖	noodle	面条
drink	饮料	rice	米饭
coffee	咖啡	chicken	鸡肉
orange juice	橙汁	beef	牛肉
tea	茶	fish	鱼
Coke/Coca-Cola	可口可乐		

  ## Situational Conversations　情景对话

1. Taking Meals On the Flight　机上用餐

(A: Cabin Attendant; B: Passenger)

Scene 1

A: Do you need anything to drink, sir?

B: What kind of drinks do you have?

A: We have coffee, tea, juice, coke, spirit and water.

B: Coffee, please.

A: With milk?

B: Yes, please. How much longer does it take to get to Paris?

A: In less than five hours. We are on time.

B: That's great. I'm anxious about my connecting flight. Do you have any Chinese newspaper?

A: Yes, we have, sir. We have China Daily. Do you want a copy?

B: Yes, please. And please get me some more coffee?

A: All right. Just a moment, please.

Scene 2

A: Excuse me. It is time for dinner. Would you mind putting down the tray?

B: Never mind.

A: We have Curried Chicken with Rice and Stewed Beef with Noodle[①]. Which one do you prefer?

B: Chicken with Rice, please.

A: Fine. Would you like something to drink? We've got whisky, brandy, red wine, beer, fruit juice and mineral water.

B: A glass of red wine, please.

A: OK. Anything else?

B: Can I have some coffee, please?

A: Coffee will be served in a few minutes[②].

B: Thank you.

Scene 3

B: Excuse me, Miss. Could you get us something to drink, please?

A: Certainly, sir. But there's a charge for alcoholic beverages in economy class. Would you refer to this price list, please? And then give me your order.

B: That's not necessary, Miss. I just want a Coke.

A: All right. There'll be no charge for soft drinks.

B: Could I purchase a snack? I'm hungry.

A: Let me give you some peanuts, and dinner will be served soon.

B: It's very considerate of you③.

2. Taking Care of the Tourists Who Are Not Feeling Well 照顾不适游客

(A: Cabin Attendant; B: Tour Leader; C: Tourist)

Scene 1

A: I see your seat light is on. May I help you, sir?

B: Yes. One of our group members is not feeling well.

A: What seems to be the problem?

B: He had a bad headache. Do you have any aspirin?

A: I'll call our doctor for him. Just a moment, please.

B: And this lady is having trouble with her chair④. Can you help her?

A: I'm sorry, ma'am. I'll push the button, and you pull it forward, please.

C: Thank you. May I unfasten my seat belt now?

A: Yes, ma'am, but we suggest you wear it loosely buckled⑤.

Scene 2

A: What can I do for you, sir?

B: Excuse me, Miss. A member of our tour group feels like vomiting. Can I bother you for some iced water, please?

A: Certainly, sir. But can I suggest a glass of hot water instead? I think it may help settle down his stomach⑥.

B: Yes, please.

A: He can find an airsick bag in the seat pocket in front of him, if he needs it.

B: Thank you very much for your kindness.

A: That's all right. I'll be back with the water in a minute.

B: Thank you so much.

Scene 3

B: Excuse me, Miss. Would you please give us some blankets? Some tourists of our group feel a little bit cold.

A: Sure. I will get some for you. By the way, did you turn off the airflow overhead?

B: Yes, I did. But I still feel cold.

A: I will be back with the blanket shortly.

B: One more thing to bother you. This lady's earphones are not working.

A: Let me check them, ma'am. Can you hear anything now?

C: Yes, but it's too loud.

B: Please adjust the volume. The volume control switch is right here.

C: I see. Thank you very much for your help.

3. Asking for In-flight Services　要求机上服务

(A: Cabin Attendant; B: Tour Leader; C: Tourist)

Scene 1

A: What can I do for you?

B: Do you have a bassinet, Miss?

A: Certainly. Would you like one, sir?

B: Yes. This lady of our group has a baby. She needs one for the baby to sleep in.

A: Here you are, ma'am.

C: Thank you.

A: It's my pleasure. We also have diapers, bottles, formula milk, and baby food[⑦]. If you need anything during the flight, please let me know.

C: It's very kind of you. Bring me some diapers, please.

A: Just a moment, please. I'll come back right away.

C: Thank you very much indeed.

Scene 2

(A: Cabin Attendant; B: Passenger)

A: Excuse me, ma'am. We are passing through some turbulence right now. Would you please fasten your seat belt?

B: Yes, but I don't feel very well. Can I have two more pillows, please?

A: Sure. Do you think you need any medicine?

B: I am probably a little airsick. Some pills might be helpful.

A: OK. I'll bring the pills right away. By the way, dinner will be served in 20 minutes. Do you want to be served for later?

B: No. I don't think that will be necessary. Could you tell me what we will have tonight?

A: You may choose chicken with steamed rice or beef curried with noodles?

B: Sounds great.

A: It is. Would you like something to drink in advance? We have all kinds of soda, juice, beer and wine.

B: Thanks. You are very thoughtful. I think I could use some apple juice right now.

A: Sure. I'll be right back. In the meantime, if you need anything, just press the service button on the arm of the seat. There will be someone here for you.

B: I got it. Thank you. Do you sell duty-free goods on this plane?

A: Yes. We do.

B: Where can I get a list of all those duty-free goods?

A: It's right in our in-flight magazine.

B: When will you start this service?

A: After the dinner is served.

4. Asking for Immigration Cards And Customs Declaration Forms 索要入境登记卡和海关申报单

(A: Cabin Attendant; B: Tour Leader)

Scene 1

A: What can I do for you, ma'am?

B: May I have some entry cards and customs declarations?

A: Certainly, ma'am. We will be handing out entry cards and customs declarations for passengers to fill out.

B: There are 20 members in our group. I'd like to get 20 cards and 20 forms. I'll fill them out.

A: Here are 20 entry cards and 20 forms. Please tell your tourists not to ask any more.

B: I see. Thank you, Miss.

A: Please fill them out before your arrival. If there is anything you don't understand, I'll be glad to help you.

B: That's very kind of you.

Scene 2

B: Excuse me, what time do you expect to land at Vienna International Airport?

A: We should be in Vienna by 10 o'clock in the evening, sir.

B: Do you have any idea how long it will take to go through the Immigration?

A: It all depends on traffic from other arriving aircraft.

B: What happens after we go through the Immigration?

A: Your next step is the baggage claim area.

B: Then what?

A: You'll go through the customs. And how long are you staying in Austria?

B: I have a one-month tourist visa. Will I be allowed to stay that long?

A: No, not necessarily. I'm afraid your length of stay will be determined by an immigration officer.

B: I didn't know that.

5. Asking for Flight Information 了解飞行信息

(A: Cabin Attendant; B: Tour Leader)

Scene 1

A: May I help you, sir?

B: Yes. What's the time difference between Beijing and London?

A: Eight hours. Beijing is eight hours ahead.

B: Are we gaining or losing a day on the way to Britain?

A: We're losing a day. So we're arriving on the same day.

B: And what's the actual time from Shanghai to London?

A: About 10 hours.

B: Can you tell me what time we'll arrive?

A: Sure. Oh, 7 o'clock in the evening, I mean local time. If you like further information on this, there's a guidebook in several languages at the information desk.

B: Do you have a Chinese edition?

A: I'm afraid we don't. Won't an English edition do?

B: I'll try to read it.

Scene 2

B: Excuse me, stewardess.

A: Yes, sir?

B: When do we arrive in Seoul?

A: We're due in Seoul at 11:30 a.m. Seoul time[8]. Our flight delayed about an hour and thirty minutes to take off on account of bad weather.

B: What time are we going to arrive?

A: About 13:00 p.m. Seoul time.

B: What's the time difference between Beijing and Seoul.

A: It's one hour. Seoul time is one hour ahead of Beijing time.

B: What's the weather like in Seoul?

A: It may be rainy. The temperature is around 10℃[9]. Please refer to the flight information on the screen[10].

B: I see. Thank you for your information.

Notes 注释

① We have Curried Chicken with Rice and Stewed Beef with Noodle. 我们有咖喱鸡饭和红烧牛肉面。

② Coffee will be served in a few minutes. 过一会儿就供应咖啡。
   serve 供应；in a few minutes 过一会儿

③ It's very considerate of you. 谢谢您。
   Considerate 体贴的，替人着想；It was very considerate of you to remember my birthday. 谢谢你记得我的生日。

④ …this lady is having trouble with her chair. 这位太太的椅子调不好。
   have trouble with… 有困难、忧虑、痛苦
   We are having trouble with our computer system. 我们的电脑系统很让人伤脑筋。

⑤ …we suggest you wear it loosely buckled. 我们建议您系着安全带，把扣扣得松一点儿。

⑥ …it may help settle down his stomach. 这样会让他的胃舒服一点。
   settle down （使）平静下来，舒适

⑦ We also have diapers, bottles, formula milk, and baby food. 我们还有尿布、奶瓶、调好的奶和婴儿食品。

⑧ We're due in Seoul at 11:30 a.m. 飞机原计划上午11:30到达汉城。

⑨ The temperatures is around 10℃. 舱外温度约10摄氏度左右。
　　10℃：ten degrees Celsius；Celsius，摄氏温标，冰点为0℃，沸点为100℃；另一种温标为 Fahrenheit 华氏温标，冰点为32℉，沸点为212℉。
　　due 　（车、船等）预定应到的；预期的；约定的
　　The train is due to leave at six. 　火车定于6点钟开出。

⑩ Please refer to the flight information. 　请参阅飞行信息。
　　refer to 　查阅，参考，查询；refer to the map 　查阅地图

Useful Sentences　必学句型

1. Excuse me, stewardess. Would you show me the way to my seat?
   对不起，空姐。你可以把我带到我的座位上吗？

2. What's your seat number?
   您的座位是几号呢？

3. My boarding pass says 11 B.
   我的登机牌是11 B。

4. Is this seat taken?
   这个座位有人吗？

5. Would you put this bag in the overhead bin for me?
   请你帮我把行李放在行李柜里好不好？

6. Excuse me. May I put my bag in this empty seat beside me?
   对不起，我可以把我的包放在我旁边的这张空座位上吗？

7. I'm sorry. All carry-on luggage must be placed underneath the seat in front of you or in the overhead compartment.
   很抱歉。所有随身携带的行李必须放在你面前的座位底下或你头顶上方的行李柜里。

8. Can I help you with your safety belt?
   我帮您系好安全带好吗？

9. Would you show me how to fasten (take off) the seat belt?
   可以告诉我如何系紧（松开）座位安全带吗？

10. May I put my seat back?
    我可以调回座位吗？

11. Where is the button that controls my chair? Right here on the arm rest.
    控制我椅子的按钮在哪里？就在扶手上。

12. Excuse me, sir. We are passing through some turbulence right now. Would you please fasten your seat belt?
    抱歉，先生。飞机现在正经过一阵乱流，请系紧您的座位安全带好吗？

13. Will you show me how to turn on the light?
    你可以告诉我怎么开灯吗?
14. Miss, could I have a blanket and pillow, please?
    小姐,可以给我枕头和毛毯吗?
15. May I use the lavatory now?
    现在可以使用盥洗室吗?
16. When are we going to be landing?
    我们什么时候开始降落?
17. How long is the flight to Bangkok?
    到曼谷需飞行多长时间?
18. You can't hear music until takeoff.
    你要等到起飞之后才可以听音乐。
19. Please be seated until the plane comes to a complete stop.
    飞机完全停稳前,请勿离座。
20. Do you carry duty-free goods on this plane?
    机上卖免税商品吗?
21. I need a earphone.
    我需要一副耳机。
22. Which is the movie channel?
    电影频道是哪一个?
23. I'm afraid I'm not feeling very well.
    我怕是有点不舒服。
24. What kind of soft drink would you like to have, sir?
    您要喝点什么,先生?
25. What kind of juice do you have?
    你们有什么果汁?
26. What would you like, beef or chicken?
    您要哪一种,牛排还是鸡肉?
27. Could I have vegetarian dish?
    可否给我素食餐?
28. May I have some more coffee?
    请你再给我一些咖啡好吗?
29. Some coffee might help.
    喝点咖啡可能有帮助。
30. I'd like to save my lunch for later.
    我想把午餐延后,待会儿再吃。

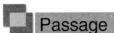 **Passage Reading**　阅读材料

Tourism

The history of tourism began with the tavern and inn of early days. They offered food and shelter to travelers. The food was usually simple and the travelers had to share beds with other travelers. The service was friendly, but the accommodations lacked the comfort and convinence travelers expect today.

Travel has always been considered to be of help to increase one's knowledge and broaden one's mind. The rapid development of the airline industry allows the public to travel to remote places. People are spending more time and money on both internal and international tours. People travel for different purposes.

People may travel entirely for sightseeing. They are often holiday tourists. People may travel around the world for business sake. They include businessmen, government officials and professional personnel attending meetings. People may travel to visit friends or relatives. Other people may travel for improving their health. Most of them are sick or elderly persons. They prefer to find a quiet and clean place for a short stay instead of touring here and there.

The fast growth of tourist industry has greatly facilitated many countries' development of national economy. In modern China, tourist industry is gaining more and more attention and it has been one of the fastest-growing industries in recent years.

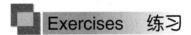 **Exercises**　练习

1. **Reading and Translation**

Traveling by Plane

At your final destination, you'd better examine your baggage for damage. If your baggage has been damaged, you can go immediately to the airline agent and demand the expense of repair.

In this case, you will have to fill out a form. And be specific when describing the damage. If the airline should lose your baggage, report the loss to the airline agent. The agent will be responsible for your loss.

Don't worry about your baggage if it is heavy and you can't manage it. Porters are available at many airports. These people will carry your bags for you, though not free of charge.

In case you are bumped from a flight for which you have a reserved ticket, and you were at the airport for check-in before closing time, the airlines must pay you money unless they can get you a seat by bargaining with another passenger. If you have a confirmed reservation, and arrive at the airport on time, and you are bumped, you can ask for a written explanation of your rights. This will explain the procedure for obtaining the money.

2. **Complete the Following Dialogues in English with the hints given in Chinese**

（1）（A：Stewardess；B：Tourist）

A：您要喝什么?

B：_____

A：有橘子汁、柠檬汽水、可口可乐、百事可乐及矿泉水。

B：_____

A：茶还是咖啡？

B：_____

A：加牛奶吗？

B：_____

A：还要咖啡吗？

B：_____

A：好的，先生。马上给您拿来。

（2）（A：Tour Leader；B：Passenger）

A：打扰一下，您介意和这位女士换一下座位吗？

B：_____

A：哦，谢谢您。你可真好。

B：_____

（3）（A：Tour Leader；B：Passenger）

A：打扰了，从这儿到纽约的实际飞行时间是多少？

B：_____

A：你能告诉我到达的时间吗？

B：_____，我指的是当地时间。

3. Role-play

Situation A

You are a tour leader traveling by air with your group. One of your group members is not feeling well. You ask a stewardess to help him. Make up a dialogue between you and a stewardess.

Situation B

You are a tour leader traveling with your group members on the plane. It's time for dinner. You help a lady to order food for her dinner. Make a dialogue between you and the stewardess who is serving dinner.

Unit 4 At the Hotel
在酒店

本课导读

入住酒店时，领队应首先与地接社导游一起，与总台确认房间数目与类型，与行李员交接行李送房事项，为团队办理入住手续。办好入住手续后，领队要与总台确定用餐的时间和地点，并通知到游客。酒店大多提供各类设施与服务方便房客使用，领队应协助地陪向游客详细介绍开放时间和收费情况。如游客在要求送餐、洗衣等服务时遇到语言障碍，领队要帮助他们联系、落实。入住期间，如游客遇到设备损坏、服务不周等各种问题，领队应及时与酒店有关部门交涉，尽力为游客解决问题。退房前一天，要通知游客整理好行李，并与行李房主管确认收行李的时间和行李件数；与总台确认旅游团的额外费用；并通知总台安排好叫醒电话和早餐。退房时，要仔细查核付款项目，交费后索取收据。离店前，应和地陪一起，清点人数和行李，确认一切无误后方可开车。

Special Terms 专业词汇

hotel	饭店	cashier	收银员，出纳员
commercial hotel	商务饭店	receptionist	接待员
resort hotel	旅游胜地饭店	floor attendant	楼层服务员
apartment hotel	公寓饭店	room maid	打扫客房的女服务员
Luxury (5-star)	五星	bellboy/bellman	行李员
High comfort (4-star)	四星	reservation	预约；预订
Average comfort (3-star)	三星	book	预订
Some comfort (2-star)	二星	vacancy	空房
Economy (1-star)	一星	vacant room	空的房间
reception	接待处	room rate	房价
front desk	前台	voucher	凭证，券
housekeeping department	房务部，管家部	single room	单人房
food and beverage department	餐饮部	double room	双人房
		twin room	双床间
entertainment department	娱乐部	triple room	三人房
resident manager	客房经理	suite	套房
duty manager	值班经理	lobby	大堂
lobby manager	大堂经理	banquet room	宴会厅
supervisor	主管	restaurant	餐厅
captain	领班	coffee shop	咖啡厅

cafeteria	自助餐厅	key card	钥匙卡
health center	健身房	laundry service	洗衣服务
sauna	桑拿浴室	laundry list	洗衣单
massage parlor	按摩室	laundry bag	洗衣袋
beauty parlor	美容室	laundry charge	洗衣费
barber shop	理发室	express service	快洗服务
tennis court	网球场	dry cleaning	干洗
bowling alley	保龄球场	press	熨衣服
billiard room	桌球室	express service charge	快件收费
mahjong and chess room	棋牌室	50% extra charge	加收50%
souvenir shop	纪念品商店	blouse	女上衣
fire exit	火警出口	coat	女短大衣
bathroom	(客房内的)洗澡间	dress	连衣裙
shower	淋浴	panties	女短裤
shower curtain	浴帘	nightdress	女睡衣
shower head	淋浴喷头	underpants	男短裤
toilet	抽水马桶	pajama	男睡衣
refrigerator	电冰箱	shirt	男衬衣
Pay-TV	收费电视	jacket	外套,短上衣
safe-box	保险箱	zipper	拉链
wall lamp	壁灯	button	纽扣
television remote control	电视遥控开关	clothes hanger	衣架
discount	折扣	hair dryer	干发机
service charge	服务费	shoe shining paper	擦鞋纸
extra charge	额外费用	towel	毛巾
sold out	卖完了	toothbrush	牙刷
fully booked	全被订满	toothpaste	牙膏
check in	入住	shampoo	洗发液
check out	结账离店,退房	shower cap	浴帽
arrival time	到达时间	cotton swabs	棉签
departure time	离开时间	toilet soap	香皂
settle accounts	结账	toilet paper	卫生纸

 Situational Conversations   情景对话

1. Checking in At the Front Desk   办理入住手续

Scene 1

(A: Receptionist; B: Tour Leader)

A: Good evening, sir. What can I do for you?

Unit 4 At the Hotel 在酒店

B: We are the tour group from China International Travel Service. My name is Li Gang. Our company made a reservation for 10 twin rooms and 1 single room four week ago.

A: Just a minute, please, Mr. Li. I'll check our reservation records. China International Travel Service. I'm sorry, there is no reservation from your service.

B: Could you check again a reservation for Friday for the tour group from Hangzhou?

A: Oh, yes. You had reserved 10 twin rooms and 1 single room for three days from July 3rd to 6th.

B: Yes, exactly.

A: Can I see your passports, please, sir?

B: Certainly, Miss. Here is the name list and passports of our group.

A: Thank you, sir. And please fill in the registration forms.

B: All right.

A: How are you going to pay, in cash or credit card?

B: Do you accept traveler's checks?

A: Certainly, sir. Here are the keys to your rooms. Please make sure that you have them with you all the time. You'll be required to show them when you sign for your meals and drinks in the restaurants and bars. The bellmen will show you up to your rooms.

B: Thanks a lot.

Scene 2

(A: Receptionist; B: Tour Leader; C: Local Guide)

A: Good morning, sir. May I help you?

C: Good morning. My name is Peter Smith. I'm the local guide of the United Travel Service.

A: Just a moment, sir. I'll check the reservation list. Yes, we are holding 15 twins for two nights for you.

C: That's right, but there is a change. Can we have 14 twins and 2 single rooms instead?

A: Yes, we do have single rooms at the moment. But you'll have to pay for the other single.

B: I see. What's the room rate?

A: The daily rate for a single room is $120 per night. You are going to stay from the 18th to 20th. That's two nights.

B: OK. Here is $240.

A: Thank you.

B: Then that's settled. Thank you, Peter Smith.

C: My pleasure.

A: Could I see your group visa, please?

B: Yes, sure. Here you are.

A: Thank you. Here are the registration cards. Please help your tour members fill them in.

B: Sure. Thank you.

A: It's my pleasure. Here are the room keys for your group. I hope you'll enjoy your stay at our hotel.

B: Thank you. I'm sure we will.

C: Is everything all right?

B: Yes. I have distributed all the keys among the tour members. Here is a copy of the name list for you. How about our luggage?

C: Don't worry. Your luggage will be sent to your rooms immediately.

2. Confirming the Wake-up Call and Luggage Check-out Time 与总台确定叫醒时间和收行李的时间

(A: Receptionist; B: Tour Leader)

A: Good afternoon. Can I help you, sir?

B: Good afternoon. I'm Zhou Li, the tour leader from the Hangzhou China Travel Service.

A: Welcome to our hotel.

B: Thank you.

A: You've made a reservation for 20 twin rooms for today, November 18th. Am I correct?

B: Well, I'm afraid we've had some last minute change[①]. I need a connecting room for a family of five[②].

A: I'm sorry we don't have any more connecting rooms. Could I suggest a suite instead?

B: What about the rate?

A: As it is a family suite, it will cost the same as the two rooms.

B: Great! I take it.

A: Your check-out-time is at 8:00 tomorrow morning. Has there been any change in your schedule?

B: Yes. We'd like to change our check-out-time to 8:30 a.m.

A: 8:30 a.m. Certainly, sir. And is there any change in the number of your group?

B: Yes, I'm just going to talk about this with you. There are 40 people in our group, and we are leaving tomorrow morning. But a couple won't go with the group. They'll have to remain for another couple of days. Can they keep the same room?

A: What's their room number, please?

B: 708.

A: Well, let me see. (Checks the list) Yes, they can.

B: Very good.

A: So you are staying here for one night and you'll check out at 8:30 a.m. tomorrow morning.

B: Exactly. Would you please give us a morning call at 6:45 tomorrow morning?

A: Certainly, sir. A morning call at 6:45 tomorrow morning and your luggage will be collected at 7:45. Will that be all right?

B: Yes.

A: Here are the registration cards. Please help your guests fill them in. Thank you very much.

B: Don't mention it. Thank you.

A: Would you please sign your name here, sir? Thank you. Here are the room keys. Is there anything else we can do for you, sir?

B: No, not at the moment. Thank you very much indeed.

A: Glad to be of service.

3. Inquiring About Telephone Service   询问电话服务

Scene 1

(A: Operator; B: Tourist)

A: This is the operator. May I help you?

B: Yes. What's my telephone number?

A: The extension number is just the same as your room number.

B: And I'd like to call my local guide in his room. What should I do?

A: Do you know the room number, sir?

B: Yes. It's 536.

A: Please dial 20 and then the room number.

B: I see. I also want to make a local call. Can you tell me how to make it?

A: Certainly, sir. Please dial 9 for outside call first and followed by area code and the number you want.

B: May I know the area code in your country?

A: There is a telephone directory in the drawer of the writing desk. You may refer to it.

B: Thank you very much for your help.

A: You are welcome, sir. If you have any questions, please call me. Have a nice day.

Scene 2

(A: Operator; B: Tourist; C: Receptionist)

A: Operator. May I help you?

B: Yes. I'd like to make a call back to China.

A: Certainly, sir. May I know your room number?

B: Room 1218, Mr. Li.

A: Mr. Li, you should put a deposit in the front desk first. Then I'll make international calls for you.

B: How much for the deposit?

A: I'm not very clear about it. You can contact with the front desk. Hold on, please. I'll put you through to the front desk[③].

(At the front desk)

C: Front Desk, can I help you?

B: Yes, I'm in Room 1218. My name is Li Gang. I'd like to make IDD call in my room[④].

C: All right, Mr. Li. But we require a deposit of 100 dollars for the telephone charge.

B: No problem. I'll come to pay the deposit right away.

(At the front desk)

C: Good afternoon, sir. May I help you?

B: Yes. I'm Li Gang in Room 1218. Here is a deposit of 100 dollars.

C: Thank you, Mr. Li. This is the receipt for the deposit. Please keep it. You can make international calls at your room in 5 minutes.

(In Room 1218)

A: This is operator, Mr. Li. Your international call has been connected. Go ahead, please.

B: But I wonder how to dial.

A: Please dial 00 first, and then the country code, the area code and the number you want.

B: Thank you very much.

A: It's our pleasure.

Scene 3

A: This is the operator. May I help you?

B: Yes, I'd like to have a morning call tomorrow morning.

A: At what time shall we call you?

B: At 6:00 a.m. We are a group from Hangzhou China Travel Service. Our group is to take the early flight to Shanghai tomorrow morning. Please give wake-up calls for Room 1101, 1102, 1103, 1105 and 1106 at 6:00 a.m., that's five rooms altogether.

A. I see. Wake-up calls for Room 1101, 1102, 1103, 1105 and 1106 at 6:00 tomorrow morning.

B: That's right.

A: We have a computer wake-up service at each room[⑤]. Please dial 5 first and then the time. That is to say, dial 5 and then 0600 for the time. There must be five digits in the final number.

B: If I want to change my wake-up time, what should I do?

A: Just dial your new wake-up time. The computer will cancel the old time and record the new one.

B: Will I be woken up at 6:30 a.m. if I dial 50630?

A: Yes, that is right.

B: I see. Thank you very much for your help.

A: It's our pleasure to serve you.

4. Asking for Hotel Services 要求店内服务

Scene 1

(A: Floor Attendant; B: Tourist)

A: Housekeeping. May I come in?

B: Yes, come in.

A: Good evening, sir. Did you call for service?

B: Yes. The air conditioner doesn't work.

A: I'm sorry, sir. A repairman will come and check it right away.

B: One more thing. Do you have larger size slippers than the ones that I have in my room? They are too small for me.

A: I'm not really sure, sir. But I'll try and see if I can get you a pair of larger ones. Anything else I can do for you?

B: I need a couple more of clothes hangers.

A: I'll fetch you some right away. Is four hangers enough?

B: Yes. That's more than enough. Thank you.

Scene 2

(A: Floor Attendant; B: Tourist)

A: Housekeeping. May I help you?

B: Yes. I have some laundry to be done.

A: Well, would you fill in the laundry form, please?

B: May I know where the form is?

A: The laundry bag and laundry form are in the drawer of the writing desk.

B: Would you please send someone to pick up my laundry?

A: Yes, ma'am. I'll send someone immediately. Just put your laundry in the laundry bag.

(A few minutes later)

A: Housekeeping. May I come in?

B: Yes. Come in, please.

A: Good morning, ma'am. I come to collect your laundry.

B: When can I have my laundry back?

A: Usually in a day. If you send your laundry before 10:00 in the morning, it will be ready by the evening.

B: What is the price?

A: The price is printed on the laundry form. If you want express service, we'll deliver it within four hours at a 50% extra charge.

B: I see.

Scene 3

(A: Head Waiter of the Room Service; B: Tourist)

A: Room service. May I help you?

B: Yes. I'd like to have my breakfast in my room tomorrow morning. Could you send it here? I'm in Room 1512.

A: Certainly, sir. We provide very good room service. What would you like?

B: I'd like to have a full breakfast⑥.

A: What kind of juice would you like?

B: Orange juice.

A: Would you like sausage, bacon or ham?

B: Sausage, please.

A: How would you like your eggs, sir, fried or boiled?

B: Two fried eggs, sunny-side up⑦.

A: Very well, sir. So that's orange juice, sausage and eggs, sunny-side up.

B: That's right. By the way, is there any other way to have room service?

A: Yes, sir. Just check the items you would like for breakfast in your doorknob menu, mark down the time and hang it outside your door before you go to bed.

A: But what should we do with the dishes when we finish our breakfast?

B: Please leave them outside your room. The waiter will come to collect them.

A: I see. Thank you very much for your service.

5. Luggage Collection 收行李

(A: Local Guide; B: Tour Leader; C: Bell Captain)

A: Ladies and gentlemen, attention please. We are going to check out early tomorrow morning. Would you please have your bags ready by 10:30 tonight, and leave them right outside the door? We are going to check them. I have also arranged an early morning call for you. It's at 6:00 a.m. Breakfast will be served at 6:30. Since the departure time of the flight is 8:30 a.m., we have to set off at 7:00. If you have any problem, please don't hesitate to let me know.

A: (To the tour leader) Shall we meet on the 18th floor five minutes before 10:30 tonight? We will be there together to check the luggage.

B: Certainly. You're very considerate.

(At 10:30 p.m. on the 18th floor where the tour group is staying)

B: We've got 32 pieces of luggage altogether.

A: Let me see. Oh, this one has no lock on it. It's Mr. Chen's, I think. According to the regulations of the airline, all bags must be locked except the carry-on luggage. Otherwise, they will not be accepted.

B: I'll tell Mr. Chen to lock it.

(The bag has been locked)

A: Everything is fine, Mr. Li. We can hand over the luggage to the bellboy now.

B: Yes, certainly.

(A is making a call to the Bell Captain's Desk)

C: This is the Bell Captain's Desk. May I help you?

A: Yes. We are going to check out early tomorrow morning. Could you pick up our luggage, please?

C: Certainly, sir. May I have your room number, please?

A: It's on the 18th floor. Room 1801 to Room 1814, Room 1821 and 1822. Sixteen rooms altogether.

C: All right, sir. (A few minutes later) Good evening, sir. I've come for your bags.

B: Thank you. Could you take down our luggage? There are 20 pieces altogether.

C: Is there anything valuable or breakable in them?

B: No.

C: This is your claim tag, sir. We'll keep our luggage at the Bell Captain's Desk. Could you pick it up there tomorrow morning, please?

B: Certainly, thank you very much.

C: It's our pleasure to serve you.

6. Checking Out 结账离店

Scene 1

(A: Front Desk Cashier; B: Tour Leader)

A: Good morning! Can I help you?

B: I'd like to check out for our group.

A: May I have your name and room number, please?

B: My name is Charley Chen, the tour leader from CTS, Zhejiang. We stay in Room 1515 to Room 1518, four rooms altogether.

A: Yes, Mr. Chen. You came here three days ago on December 6th, didn't you?

B: Yes, Miss.

A: Just a moment, please. I'll draw up your bill for you[8]. Your bill totals 880 dollars, Mr. Chen. Would you like to check it? The telephone charge for Room 1516 hasn't been paid yet.

B: Yes. Telephone charges will be paid individually[9]. Maybe the guest in Room 1516 forgets to come here to clear his bill. Just a minute, please. I'll inform him.

A: Thank you, Mr. Chen. Would you sign on the bill, please?

B: Certainly. Here you are.

A: Thank you. Mr. Chen. Here is your receipt. Hope to serve you again next time.

B: Thank you for your service.

Scene 2

(A: Tour Leader; B: Local Guide; C: The Whole Group; D: Cashier)

A: Good morning, everyone. We are going to check out this morning. Is everybody here? And is everybody's luggage ready?

C: Yes.

A: Thank you for being so punctual. The bellmen will take your luggage to the bus. Ten minutes later, we'll meet at the coffee shop. Breakfast is to be served at 7:30. After the breakfast, let's meet on the bus. We'll set off to the airport at 8:10. The departure time of the flight is 10 o'clock this morning. Is this schedule all right?

C: Yes, thank you.

A: (To the local guide) would you please come with me to check the luggage, Mr. Brown?

B: Yes, certainly.

A: There are altogether 12 pieces of luggage.

B: Are they all locked?

A: Yes, they are. Now, shall we go to the front desk to check out?

B: Certainly.

D: Good morning, would you like to check out?

A: Yes, our rooms are 601, 602, 603, 604, 605 and 606. My name is Li Gang.

D: Here is your bill. Please have a check. The total amount including the meal charge is 3 000 dollars. Is that right?

A: Yes. I think so.

D: Would you please sign on the bill, Mr. Li?

A: Certainly, Miss. Here you are.

D: Thank you, Mr. Li. Here is your receipt. Hope you've enjoyed your stay in our hotel.

Notes 注释

① I'm afraid we've had some last minute change. 恐怕我们有一些最新变化。

② I need a connecting room for a family of five. 一个五口之家需要一间相通房间。
connecting room 相通房, adjoining room 相连房

③ I'll put you through to the front desk. 我替你将电话转到总台。

④ I'd like to make IDD call in my room. 我想在房内打国际长途。
IDD call: International Direct Dial call 国际长途直拨电话

⑤ We have a computer wake-up service at each room. 我们饭店每个房间都有电脑叫醒服务。

⑥ full breakfast (American breakfast) 美式早餐, 比欧洲大陆式早餐丰盛, 通常有果汁、咖啡、香肠（熏肉或火腿）、鸡蛋和面包或烤面包片。

⑦ sunny-side up 单面煎; easy over or fried over 双面煎。

⑧ I'll draw up your bill for you. 我给你开列账单; draw up 写出, 制订。

⑨ Telephone charges will be paid individually. 话费由客人自付。
individually 以个人资格; 分别地, 各个地; 各自地

  Passage Reading   阅读材料

Classification of Hotels

A hotel is a contemporary home for people who are traveling. Taverns in the old days offered food and shelters to travelers. In a modern hotel, the travelers can rest and have access to food and drink. More often, the hotel may also offer facilities for recreation, such as a swimming pool, a tennis court, a billiard room, a dancing hall, etc.

Generally speaking, hotels can be classified into 4 categories according to the variation of their clients. The first is the commercial hotel, which accommodates people who mainly travel on business. The second is the resort hotel, which serves tourists who travel for enjoyment. The third is the convention hotel which aims its services largely at the convention trade. The fourth is the resident hotel, which caters to people who do not want to keep house themselves and rent accommodations on a seasonal basis or even permanently.

No firm distinction exists among the different kinds of hotels. One hotel may offer all kinds of services mentioned above. A small motel——an accommodation which permits automobile parking near the guests' rooms——may have banquet rooms and meeting rooms as well as its accommodations. Many resort hotels nowadays are also equipped with complete convention facilities.

Exercises 练习

1. Reading and Translation

Different Eating Habits

Different nations have different ways of cooking, serving and eating. For example, the British usually have an afternoon tea or high tea consisting of tea and some refreshments like cookie or biscuit. The British and the Americans like to eat raw vegetables and have their meat half-done. They usually do not eat the meat of dogs. As to the table manners, usually they can not appreciate the Chinese way of picking dishes for their guests which show their hospitality. That may be considered unsanitary.

Some Western Manners

(1) It is considered bad manners in the West to leave on one's plate.

(2) Do not refuse the offer of food or drink when in fact you are still hungry or thirsty.

(3) If you want something, ask for it.

(4) If you do not want something, just say, "No, thanks. I just don't feel like it. I' take some…"

Handling Silverware

At a dinner with the Europeans, hold the knife in the right hand, the fork in the left, and manage the knife and fork with both hands. Keep your knife and fork in your hands until you finish eating. They have their coffee after the meal.

When eating with the Americans, you can use just one hand whenever possible and keep the other hand on your lap. Use your fork in the right hand to pick up, for instance, the pieces of tomatoes. When you have to cut or slice the meat, you can change your fork to your left hand and pick up your knife in the right hand to cut the meat. Then you can put your knife down and change your fork to your right hand to pick up the sliced meat. Then, perhaps, you'll suddenly think of your coffee or orange juice. So put down your fork to drink the coffee. Busy as you are, it is acceptable.

2. Complete the Following Dialogues in English with the hints given in Chinese

(1) (A: Room Attendant; B: Tour Leader)

A: 你需要帮助吗?

B: _____

A: 真对不起,先生。修理人员很快就会来检查的。

B: _____

(2) (A: Operator; B: Tour Leader)

A: 这里是话务员,可以为您效劳吗?

B: _____ 叫醒我。

A: 几点钟?

B: _____

(3) (A: Tourist; B: Room Attendant)

A: _____

B：请先填一下洗衣单。

A：_____

B：洗衣单在写字台的抽屉里。

3. **Role-play**

Situation A

You are a tour leader. You just arrived at Paris with your group. You are now checking in at the Hilton Hotel. Make up a dialogue between you and the receptionist of the hotel.

Situation B

You take a group of Europe Tour in Paris. You are leaving the hotel to catch a morning flight back to Shanghai. Make a speech to your group members about the check-out, and then check out for your group with the front desk cashier.

Unit 5　Money Exchanging　货币兑换

本课导读

境外旅游时，携带一定数量的外币是必要的。中国旅游者出国往往携带大量的外币现金，但这样既不安全又不方便。领队在出国前应尽量劝导游客办理国际信用卡，持信用卡消费，既方便又安全，持卡人可在商户 POS 机上刷卡消费，也可在 ATM 机上查询、提取现金。每到一地，领队应及时了解当地的汇率，带游客去汇率较高的银行兑换当地货币，尽力为游客换汇提供方便。

Special Terms　专业词汇

bank teller	银行职员	draft	汇票
account	账户	interest	利息
saving account	储蓄存款账户	buying rate	买入汇率，买价
checking account	支票账户	selling rate	卖出汇率，卖价
payee	收款人	denomination	面额
payer	付款人	exchange rate	汇率
bankbook	存折	withdraw	取款
deposit	存款	exchange	兑换（钱、支票）
check/cheque	支票	CNY ¥	人民币
traveler's check	旅行支票	USD $	美元
personal check	个人支票	GBP £	英镑
cash	现金	Euro EUR	欧元
to cash a check	用支票兑换现金	Thai Bahts	泰铢
credit card	信用卡	coin	硬币
American Express Card	运通卡	currency exchange receipt	货币兑换收据
Visa Card	维萨卡	money exchange memo	兑换水单
Master Card	万事达卡	place of issue	票据签发地点
foreign currency	外币	date of issue	票据签发日期

Situational Conversations　情景对话

1. Inquiring About the Exchanging Rate　询问外币兑换率

(A: Bank Teller; B: Tourist)

Scene 1

A: Good morning. May I help you?

B: Yes. I'd like to change some American dollars into Japanese yen, please.

A: Certainly. How much would you like to change?

B: Two hundred dollars. What's the exchange rate for American currency today?

A: It's 8 150 Japanese yen for 100 US dollars.

B: By the way, how about the exchange rate of USD for EUR today?

A: Our buying rate is 130.6 US dollars for 100 Euros.

B: Thank you. Here is 200 dollars.

A: Would you please fill in the declaration form[①]? Just a moment, please, sir.

Scene 2

A: Can I help you, sir?

B: I was told that foreign currency could be converted at this bank.

A: That's right. What are you going to convert, bank notes or traveler's check?

B: I'd like to convert some US dollars into Australian dollars. Could you tell me the current rate for US dollars, please?

A: With pleasure, sir. It's 76.23 US dollars for 100 Australian dollars.

B: Do you accept traveler's checks?

A: Yes, we do.

B: Shall I sign them?

A: Yes, please. What notes do you want?

B: Give me small notes, fives and tens, please.

A: Here you are, please have a check. And here is your exchange memo.

B: Thank you.

Scene 3

B: Excuse me, do you exchange foreign money?

A: Sorry, sir. We don't deal in foreign currency.

B: Could you tell me where I can exchange my dollars for Thai Bahts?

A: You can do it at Bank of Thailand.

(At Bank of Thailand)

A: What can I do for you, sir?

B: I'd like to exchange some CNY for Thai Bahts.

A: What's the amount you'd like to exchange?

B: I'd like to exchange ￥100. What's the exchange rate today?

A: Today's rate for cash purchases is 100 CNY for 466 THB in notes.

B: That's all right. Here is the money.

2. Exchanging US Dollars into Local Currency 兑换外币

(A: Bank Teller; B: Tour Leader; C: Tourist)

Scene 1

A: Good morning, sir. Can I help you?

B: Yes. This lady needs some Australian dollars. Would you please change them for her?

A: Certainly, ma'am. What kind of foreign currency have you got?

C: US dollars. What's today's exchange rate for US dollars?

A: It is 97.2 Australian dollars for 100 US dollars.

C: I want to change 500 dollars.

A: That is 486 USD in all. Would you please fill in the currency exchange declaration form?

C: Leader, can you help me with it?

B: Certainly, ma'am, with pleasure. Here you are.

C: Here is 500 dollars.

A: Thank you. What denominations would you like?

C: What does "denomination" mean, leader?

B: How would you like your money?

C: I would like four 100-dollar bills, five 10-dollar bills, and coins for the rest amount.

A: Would you please sign on the memo?

C: Sure.

A: Thank you, ma'am. Here are your money and exchange memo. Please keep the memo. It may come in handy later on②. And here is your declaration form.

B: Thank you ever so much.

A: It's my pleasure.

Scene 2

B: Excuse me. I'd like to cash the balance of my traveler's L/C and change them into Japanese yen③.

A: May I have the L/C and your passport, please?

B: Certainly. Here you are.

A: Please fill in the receipt in duplicate④, put down the amount in Arabic figures⑤ as well as in words, and also the name of the issuing bank, the number of the credit and the date of issue, and finally please sign your name here.

B: Thank you. Here you are.

A: The balance is 356 US dollars. Today's exchange rate for Japanese yen is 81.5 yen for 100 dollars. The total amount is 29020 JPY. Here is your money. Please have a check, sir.

B: Thank you.

A: Will you please sign the exchange memo? Please keep the memo in case you want to change the Japanese yen back into US dollars.

B: I see. Thank you very much.

3. Changing the Local Currency Back into US Dollars 换回美元

(A: Bank Teller; B: Tour Leader)

A: What can I do for you?

B: Some of our group members still have some Japanese yen left with them. Can we change the money back into US dollars here?

A: Are you leaving Japan?

B: Yes, Miss. We are leaving tomorrow for China by air.

A: Then, you can change them at the bank at the Narita International Airport[⑥] before boarding the plane.

B: We were told that it's very difficult to exchange foreign currencies at the airport, so we'd like to convert it back into US dollars right now.

A: All right. Please fill in the exchange memo.

B: All right, but I don't know how to fill it. Can you do me a favor?

A: Sure, sir. Please put your surname and your given name here, the currency you want to change here, your passport number and home address down here. Good, please sign your name at the bottom. All right, hand it to me. Just a moment, please.

B: Thank you very much.

A: Today's exchange rate for US dollar is 81.5 JPY for 100 USD. And 12380 JPY is for 152 US dollars. How do you like to have them?

B: Five 20-dollar bills, five 10-dollar bills and two 1-dollar coins.

A: Here is your money. Please check it.

B: Thank you.

4. Cashing Traveler's Checks 兑换旅行支票

(A: Bank Teller; B: Tourist)

A: Good morning, sir. May I help you?

B: Yes. I'd like to exchange some US dollars into Australian dollars.

A: Cash or check.

B: Traveler's check.

A: Certainly, sir. Today's exchange rate is 97.2 AUD for 100 USD.

B: OK. I want to change only 500 US dollars out of this 1 000-dollar traveler's check.

A: Could you please show me your passport?

B: Here you are.

A: Thank you, sir. Please sign the check and fill in the declaration form. 500 USD is for 486 AUD. How would you like to have them?

B: Four 100-dollar bills and eight 5-dollar bills, and coins for the rest amount, please.

A: All right. Here are four 100-dollar bills and eight 5-dollar bills, and six coins, four hundred and eighty-six dollars altogether. And here is the receipt. Is that correct?

B: Yes, thanks. Good-bye.

A: Good-bye. Enjoy your stay in Australia.

5. Drawing Money at the ATM 在自动取款机取钱

(A: Local Citizen; B: Tourist)

B: Excuse me, sir.

A: Yes? What can I do for you, ma'am?

B: I want to draw some money from the Automatic Teller Machine (ATM). But I don't know how to handle it.

A: That's rather simple. Do as you are instructed.

B: I know. But I'm afraid it may "swallow" my card.

A: That seldom occurs. If you push the right buttons, your money is drawn.

B: All right. I'll remember the instruction.

A: It's getting dark, and don't let any stranger help you even if he offers to.

B: I see. Thank you for your advice.

A: Have a nice evening. Bye.

Notes 注释

① Would you please fill in the declaration form? 请填写货币兑换申请表。

② It may come in handy later on.

   come in handy 迟早有用

③ I'd like to cash the balance of my traveler's L/C…

   balance 余额；L/C: letter of credit 信用证

④ Please fill in the receipt in duplicate…

   in duplicate 一式两份

   Prepare a report in duplicate. 准备一个报告，一式两份。

⑤ …put down the amount in Arabic figures…

   put down 写下某事

   Put down the web address in your notebook. 把这个网址记在你的笔记本里。

⑥ …you can change them at the bank at the Narita International Airport…

   Narita International Airport 日本成田国际机场

Passage Reading 阅读材料

Currency Exchange

For the convenience of travelers, a bank has opened a special currency exchange at the airport. Tourists can exchange the money of their country for the money of the country they are visiting in order to pay for taxis or buses and to tip porters in the country's currency.

Money also can be exchanged at banks and hotels. Some stores and restaurants that deal with tourists can also exchange small amounts of currency.

The value of one country's currency as compared to another country's currency is called the rate of exchange. The value changes according to world banking and market or financial conditions. Sometimes the value, or rate of exchange, changes each day. Sometimes the rate of exchange remains stable. This means it stays the same for a long time.

The rate of exchange is posted, or published, so tourists can always know what it is. Some places charge a small fee for exchanging money. Usually, a bank charges a smaller fee than a hotel does. A hotel is not in the business of changing money and does it only as a service for guests.

Tellers at the currency exchange must know and understand the rates of exchange for currencies from all over the world. They must also be able to recognize and know the denominations of many different currencies. Before they change any money, they check the rate of exchange for that day. They are careful to give this information to the travelers.

If they have some local money left before their departure, travelers are advised to keep it until they get home and exchange it there. That way they will have the local money for any last-minute expenses. For example, perhaps they will need the money for the airport departure tax.

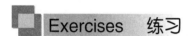

Exercises 练习

1. Reading and Translation

Subway Train

Subways are mostly found in larger cities, such as New York, London, Paris, Copenhagen, Buenos Aires, Sydney, Tokyo, and Beijing. The subway is an underground system of high speed trains. The world's first system was built in London, and trains have been operating there since 1890. Subway trains move more quickly and efficiently than buses, they will deliver you to within walking distance of almost any place in the city. They, too, are inexpensive and help solve city traffic problems. The one drawback of subway trains is that they are often crowded and noisy.

You pay your ticket by putting money into slot machines. You must select the amount of the ticket depending on the distance you will ride. The ticket will then eject from the machine. You will use the ticket for entering and exiting subway station platforms, so do not throw the ticket away. There is no person to take your ticket, only the machine.

2. Complete the Following Dialogues in English with the hints given in Chinese

(1) (A: Tourist; B: Bank Teller)

A: _____

B: 你有哪一种外币?

A: _____ 兑换美元的汇率是多少?

B: 今天的汇率是 1.6 美元兑换 1 英镑。你带了护照吗?

A: _____

B: 请在兑换水单上签字。

A: _____

(2) (A: Bank Teller; B: Tourist)

A: 晚上好, 请问有什么吩咐?

B：_____

A：当然。您要换多少？

B：_____欧元。今天的汇率是多少？

A：100 欧元兑换 140 美元。

B：_____

A：请把您的护照给我，好吗？

B：_____

A：谢谢您。请在兑换水单上签字。

B：_____

A：这是您的护照和钱，总共 280 美元，请点一下。

B：_____

A：不客气。

3. Role-play

Situation A

You are a tour leader traveling with a group in Australia. One of your group members wants to change 200 US dollars into Australian dollars. Help him and make up a dialogue between you and the bank teller.

Situation B

You are a tour leader traveling with a group in Japan. One of your group members wants to cash a USD 500 traveler's check into Japanese yen. Help her and make up a dialogue between you and the bank teller.

Unit 6 At Western Restaurants and Bar
在西餐厅和酒吧

本课导读

出境旅游团一般都会去西餐厅和酒吧感受异国风情。作为出境游的领队,必须对西餐厅和酒吧的礼仪了如指掌,在客人需要指点时,给予耐心的指导。例如在西餐厅里刀叉的正确使用方法、在食用自助餐时应当注意的礼节问题等等。除此以外,领队要熟悉西餐厅和酒吧的专业词汇以及地道的表达方法,并能进行无障碍的沟通。

Special Terms 专业词汇

bar	酒吧	measuring jug	量杯
counter	吧台	wine glass	葡萄酒杯
bar chair	酒吧椅	brandy glass	白兰地杯
barman	酒吧男招待	tumbler	平底无脚酒杯
barmaid	酒吧女招待	goblet	高脚杯
bottle opener	开瓶刀	tapering glass	圆锥形酒杯
corkscrew	酒钻	cherry	樱桃
ice shaver	削冰器	lemon	柠檬
ice maker	制冰机	clove	丁香
ice bucket	小冰桶	pineapple	菠萝
ice tongs	冰勺夹	onion	洋葱
ice scoop	冰勺	strawberry	草莓
cocktail shaker	调酒器	olive	橄榄
pouring measure	量酒器	cucumber	黄瓜
juice extractor	果汁榨汁机	mint	薄荷
electric blender	电动搅拌机	grapefruit	西柚
water jug	水壶	grape	葡萄
champagne bucket	香槟桶	soda water	苏打水
ceramic cup	陶瓷杯	rice wine	黄酒
straw	吸管	appetizer	餐前葡萄酒
decanter	酒壶	Gordon's	哥顿
mixing glasses	调酒杯	Rum	朗姆酒
beer mug	啤酒杯	Bacardi	百家得
champagne glass	香槟杯	Vodka	伏特加

Smirnoff	皇冠	lemonade	柠檬水
Whisky	威士忌	white wine	白葡萄酒
Calvados	苹果酒	red wine	红葡萄酒
Bailey's	比利酒	cider	苹果酒
Budweiser	百威啤	champagne	香槟酒
Foster's	福士啤	cocktail	鸡尾酒
Beck's	贝克啤	liqueur	白酒，烧酒
Carlsberg	加士伯啤	cognac	法国白兰地
Guinness	健力士啤	gin	琴酒
lemon juice	柠檬原汁		

Situational Conversations   情景对话

1. Paris Cocktail   巴黎式鸡尾酒

(A: Bartender; B: Tourist)

A: Good evening, madam.

B: Good evening.

A: Miss…?

B: Kate Fang.

A: Ah, yes, Miss Fang. Are you staying at our hotel?

B: Yes, I am in Room 1002.

A: Thank you, Miss Fang. Have you anything in mind as to what to drink or may I make a few suggestions?[①]

B: I have no idea about Paris cocktails.

A: Would you prefer our cocktail——Paris Cocktail? It is a mixture of real French ingredients.

B: That sounds terrific[②].

A: Here is your Paris Cocktail, Miss Fang.

B: Thank you. Oh, it tastes excellent.

A: It is a new cocktail of our hotel.

B: How do you mix it? I'd like to try it myself when I am back home.

(The bartender tells Miss Fang how to make Paris Cocktail)

B: I hope I can mix it myself. May I have my bill, please?

A: Certainly, Miss Fang. How would you like to make the payment?

B: I'd like to sign the bill.

A: All right, Miss Fang. May I have your room card, please?

B: Here you are.

A: Thank you. Miss Fang. Just a moment, please.

2. A Complaint About the Restaurant　向餐厅投诉

（A：Waiter；B：Tourist）

A：Good evening, sir. Welcome to our restaurant.

B：Good evening. I am Henry Yu.

A：Ah, Mr. Yu. This way, please.

B：Hi, boy, the dazzling lights outside the window are hurting my eyes. Could I change a table?

A：I will draw the curtains for you, sir.

B：I'd rather change a table. It is too cold here. Could you turn the air-conditioning a bit down?

A：I am sorry. I can't turn down the air-conditioning, because our hotel is central air-conditioned. Would you mind putting on your coat?

B：Well, I don't particularly care for eating with my coat on.③

A：Then, how about sitting over there?

B：There is a vacant table in the corner, where I can enjoy the band pretty well. And maybe it is warmer over there. I'd prefer the table in the corner. Can you arrange it?

A：No problem, sir. This way, please.

3. Western Breakfast　西式早餐

（A：Waiter；B：Mrs. Zhen；C：Mr. Zhen）

A：Good morning, sir and madam. What would you like to have for your breakfast?

B：What do you serve here?④

A：We serve Continental and American Breakfast.

B：What do you serve for Continental breakfast?

A：We serve rolls with butter and coffee.

B：How about American breakfast?

A：Apple juice or orange juice, tea or coffee, toast with butter or jam, eggs with bacon.

B：I will have orange juice, coffee, toast and two eggs. Can I have ham instead of bacon?

A：Certainly, madam. How would you like the eggs?

B：Easy over, Please.

A：Yes, madam. What about you, sir?

C：I will have apple juice, coffee, toast with bacon. Can I have a boiled egg, hard boiled, please?

A：Yes, sir. Orange juice, coffee, toast with ham, two eggs, and easy over for madam. Apple juice, coffee, toast with bacon and one hard boiled egg for sir. Am I correct, sir and madam?

C：Yes, thank you.

A：You are welcome.

4. At the Bar 在酒吧

(A: Bartender; B: Tourist)

A: Good evening, sir. Are you awaiting anyone?

B: No, just me.

A: Can I help you?

B: Give me a double whisky and soda.

A: Straight up, sir?

B: Certainly, without ice. Ice will spoil the taste.

A: Would you like to say "when", please, sir?

B: Whoa, When!

A: Did you have a good trip, sir?

B: Rather long and tiring.

A: Well, I wish you would have a good sleep tonight, and you will be all right tomorrow.

B: Thank you. I must be off and have a look round before dinner.

A: How about one for the road?

B: Why not? One Remy Martini V. S. O. P. no ice.⑤

A: One Remy Martini V. S. O. P. no ice, coming up immediately. Cheers, sir.

B: Will you have one yourself?

A: We are not allowed to drink on duty. Thank you all the same. But drink to your health, sir. Have a Pleasant evening and enjoy your stay with us.

5. A La Carte Dinner 点菜

(A: Waiter; B: Tour Leader; C: Miss Han)

A: Good evening, sir and madam. What would you like for your dinner, table d'hote or a la carte?

B: We would like to have a la carte.⑥

A: Here is the a la carte menu.

B: What is today's specialty?

A: We have onion soup, beef steak, lamb chop, smoked salmon and lobster.

B: What would you like, Miss Han?

C: I would like to have onion soup, a smoked salmon, a fruit salad.

A: What would you like for dessert, madam?

C: Coffee and ice cream.

A: And you, sir?

B: Onion soup, French onion soup is really good, isn't it? A beef steak and coffee.

A: How would you like the steak, sir?

B: Rare, please.

A: Would you like to have some wine with your dinner? We have very good red wine and white wine.

C: What do you suggest?

A: I would suggest Californian red wine or Chateau Haut Lafite[7] for the beef steak and Bourbon on the rocks[8] or champagne for the fish.

B: Let me have Californian red wine.

C: I will have Champagne.

A: Very well, sir and madam.

Notes 注释

① Have you anything in mind as to what to drink or may I make a few suggestions? 你们想喝点什么？我可以给你们点建议。

as to = with regard to 关于

We are puzzled as to how it happened. 关于它是如何发生的，我们很迷惑。

② That sounds terrific. 听起来棒极了！

terrific: very good or fine; splendid 极好的

③ I don't particularly care for eating with my coat on. 我不喜欢穿着外套用餐。

care for 喜欢

I don't care for tea. 我不喜欢喝茶。

④ What do you serve here? 你们提供什么餐？

⑤ One Remy Martini V. S. O. P. 人头马白兰地。

V. S. O. P.　　是储存年份的符号，表示酒龄为 20～25 年

V. O.　　　　表示酒龄为 10～12 年

V. S. O.　　　表示酒龄为 12～17 年

V. S. O. P.　　表示酒龄为 20～25 年

V. V. S. O. P.　表示酒龄为 40 年

X. O.　　　　表示酒龄为 40 年以上

⑥ a la carte 点菜

⑦ Chateau Haut Lafite 一种法国红酒

⑧ on the rocks 表示加冰块

 Passage Reading 阅读材料

Restaurant Etiquette

Etiquette is simply a set of rules that serve as tools to help you appear polished and professional. Here are a few basics that can make you go smoothly at western restaurants.

Where's my water glass? At a crowded table with several diners, it's often hard to tell which glass, napkin or coffee cup is yours. This can be especially difficult if the table is round. Solve the problem by looking at the place setting in front of you. Your liquids (water, coffee, ice tea, etc.) are always located on your right. No liquids, such as a bread plate, are always on the left.

Now that I know which water glass is mine, can I drink some? Certainly, as long as you put a napkin on your lap first. You can't eat, drink or touch food on the table without your napkin being in place. Remember, too, that it's a napkin—not a handkerchief for blowing your nose or a flag to wave for the wait staff's attention.

Where does my napkin go? There are only three places to place a napkin: (1) on your lap while you're seated at the table; (2) on the seat of your chair if you leave the table but intend to return; and (3) on the table to the right of your plate when the meal ends and you rise to leave the restaurant.

What fork do I use first? There's a simple tactic for remembering which utensils to use: begin at the outside and work toward your plate. Your salad fork is on the outside because you'll use that first. Next is the dinner fork. The fork nearest the plate is your dessert fork.

What should I do if something falls off the table? Don't panic or make a large deal out of it or get down on your knees to retrieve the fallen item. If you need a new spoon or napkin, quietly ask the wait staff for one. To go without a utensil shows bad judgment to the recruiter. (Another sign of bad judgment is to sprinkle salt or pepper on your food before tasting it. Take a bite first, and then add flavoring if needed.)

Useful Sentences　必学句型

1. Have you got a table for two, please?
   请问您有两个人的桌子吗？
2. Have you booked a table?
   您预订餐桌了吗？
3. Have you made a reservation?
   您预订了吗？
4. Smoking or non-smoking?
   吸烟区还是非吸烟区？
5. Would you like something to drink?
   您想喝什么？
6. Would you like to see the menu?
   您需要看菜单吗？
7. May I order a glass of wine?
   我可以点杯酒吗？
8. What kind of wine do you have?
   餐厅有哪几类酒？
9. I'd like to have some local wine.
   我想点当地出产的酒。
10. I'd like to have French red wine.
    我想要喝法国红酒。
11. Could you recommend some good wine?
    是否可建议一些不错的酒？

12. May I order, please?
    我可以点餐了吗?

13. What is the specialty of the house?
    餐厅最特别的菜式是什么?

14. Do you have today's speciality?
    餐厅有今日特餐吗?

15. Can I have the same dish as that?
    我可以点与那份相同的餐吗?

16. I'd like appetizers and meat (fish) dish.
    我想要一份开胃菜与排餐(鱼餐)。

17. I'm on a diet.
    我正在节食中。

18. I have to avoid food containing fat (salt/sugar).
    我必须避免含油脂(盐分/糖分)的食物。

19. Do you have vegetarian dishes?
    餐厅是否供应素食餐?

20. How do you like your steak?
    你的牛排要如何烹调?

21. Well done (medium/rare), please.
    全熟(五分熟/全生)。

Exercises 练习

1. Reading and Translation

A doll dressed in Hungarian folk costume. This is the most popular and sort of the souvenir the tourists take home with from Hungary—the colors of unique charm, the dolls' enchant. But only a few people know that not only is this wonderful item, folk doll, available on the shelf of souvenir shops among the cold walls of museums, but it is a living reality.

It is visible, tangible and can be experienced. It is a rarity, which is not disappeared in the modern life.

Holloko, possibly the most charming Hungarian village in the mountains of the northeast, is also part of the world heritage.

Local people as well as tourists can admire age-old wedding ceremonies of the polo's region. The bride's trousseau is transported along the main street for the whole world to see all the brightly decorated stuff. A sign of the family's wealth. Tradition also calls for a joined community effort to make the newly weds an anticipation for many children to come.

2. Complete the Following Dialogues in English with the hints given in Chinese

(1) (A: Tourist; B: Waitress)
(B is ordering a meal in a restaurant a few moments later)
A: 一份带汽的矿泉水。

B：_____

A：您现在可以点菜吗？

B：_____

A：是意大利蔬菜汤，可以吗？

B：_____

A：鸡肉。

B：_____

A：煮土豆。好的。

B：_____

A：好的。

（2）（A：Bartender；B：Tourist）

A：晚上好，先生。您要些什么喝的？

B：_____

A：你的酒，在这里感觉如何？一切都满意吗？

B：_____

A：很高兴听你这么说。还需要别的吗？

B：_____

A：我建议来一杯马提尼？

B：_____

A：这是您要的酒。

3. Role-Play

Situation A

You are a tour leader. You are having breakfast with a lady in your tour group in a restaurant. The lady wants to know what the restaurant serves for American breakfast. She'd like eggs easy over, ham and black coffee. The restaurant serves tea or coffee, apple juice or grapefruit juice, toast with bacon, and fried eggs. Help the lady to order. Make up a dialogue with the lady and the waitress.

Situation B

You are a tour leader. You are having a drink in a bar. You need some brandy. You ask the bartender what kinds of brandy they have. And you'd like to have a Remy Martin. The bartender greets you and tells you what they serve. Make up a dialogue between you and the bartender.

Unit 7 Shopping with Tourists 购物

本课导读

在境外购物是出境旅游中不可或缺的一个环节。一般游客会在旅游途中购物，在免税店购物，在机场办理退税，在超市购物或在百货公司购物。作为领队，不能劝说客人，甚至强迫客人在旅游途中购物。领队还要提醒客人在购物过程中索要相关票据，以免日后发生纠纷。在机场退税时，领队应能和相关人员进行基本的沟通，尽可能帮助客人解决遇到的问题。

Special Terms 专业词汇

shopping centre	商业中心区	medicated soap	药皂
department store	百货商店	detergent	洗衣粉
antique shop	古玩店	cleanser	去污粉
second-hand store	旧货店	tooth paste	牙膏
confectionery	糖果糕点	tooth brush	牙刷
cosmetics	化妆用品	toilet mirror	梳妆镜
stationery	文具	hair brush	发刷
fabrics	纺织品	compact	粉盒
dry goods	服装	powder puff	粉扑
off-the-peg	成衣	cold cream	香脂
men's wear	男服	perfume	香水
women's wear	女服	perfume spray	香水喷子
underwear	内衣裤	coat hanger	挂衣架
athletic equipment	体育用品	thread	线
sundries	零星小物	needle	针
toilet articles	盥洗用品	button	纽扣
towel	毛巾	zipper	拉链
handkerchief	手帕	key-ring	钥匙圈
toilet soap	香皂	torch, flashlight	手电
shampoo	洗发香波	bulb	灯泡
soap	肥皂	battery	电池
laundry soap	洗衣皂	lock	锁
soap powder	肥皂粉	alarm clock	闹钟
soap flakes	皂片	electric clock	电钟

Unit 7　Shopping with Tourists　购物

knapsack	背包	safety razor	保险剃须刀
handbag	女手提包	electric razor	电剃刀
briefcase/portfolio	公事包	razor blade	刀片
traveling bag	旅行包	shaving brush	剃须刷
suitcase	手提箱	shaving cream	剃须膏
trunk	大衣箱	comb	梳子
magnifying glass	放大镜	hair-net	发网
hot-water bottle	热水袋	hair pin	发夹
smoking set	烟具	hair oil/brilliantine	发油
lighter	打火机	hair lotion	生发水
baby's cot/crib	婴儿床	pomade	发膏
cradle	摇篮	hair drier	吹风机
diaper/napkin	尿布	hair-curler	卷发夹
feeding bottle/feeder	奶瓶	nail scissors	指甲剪
teat/nipple	橡皮奶嘴	nail clipper	指甲夹
dummy/comforter	假奶嘴	nail file	指甲锉
perambulator	儿童车	nail varnish/nail polish	指甲油

 Situational Conversations　情景对话

1. Shopping on the Way to Sightseeing　观光途中购物

(A: Tourist; B: Shop Assistant)

A: I want to buy some jewelry.

B: What kind of jewelry do you like to have?

A: I would like to look at some bracelets.

B: May I show you gold bracelets or platinum ones?

A: Gold ones, please.

B: Certainly, madam. Here you are.

A: What's the price for this one?

B: 550 dollars.

A: How about 500 dollars?

B: I'm sorry we only sell at fixed price.

A: OK. I'll take it. I want to have my initials engraved on it.

B: Oh, that can be done.

A: I wish to buy a diamond ring, too.

B: How many carats would you like it to be?

A: I want three carats.

B: Is this one suitable for you?

A: No, it seems too old fashioned to me.

B: What about this?

A: Let me try it on. Oh, it's too small for me, haven't you got any larger ones?

B: Yes, how about this one. It's very nice and latest in style.

A: This fits me well. Is it a real string of pearls?

B: Yes, that's genuine.

A: Will you guarantee it?

B: You may take it on my word①, if you find out it is an imitation you may return it to me.

A: What does it cost?

B: It costs 300 dollars.

A: Good, I'll take it. How much will it be altogether?

B: It comes 850 dollars.

A: Here are 900 dollars.

B: Thank you. Here are the receipt and 50 dollars change.

A: Thanks so much. You are very helpful.

B: It's my pleasure.

2. Shopping at the Duty-free Shop 在免税商店购物

(A: Shop Assistant; B: Tourist)

A: What can I do for you?

B: I'm going back to China, and I'll like to buy some real French souvenirs for my friends and relatives. I was told that I should buy some French perfumes.

A: Here we've got different brands of French perfumes. Such as Christian Dior, Lancome, Chanel, Coco, Allure, Versace, etc. You can look around and see if there is anything you like. By the way, all the products are free of duty.

B: How much does this perfume cost? It smells nice.

A: 60 dollars.

B: I think that is too dear. Can you come down a bit?

A: That's our rock bottom price②. It can not be further lowered. 60 dollars, you can't be wrong on that.③

B: OK. I'll take it.

A: Anything else?

B: Yes. I'd like a vase, and preferably something with a creamy white background.

A: How about this one?

B: It looks beautiful. How much is it then?

A: 150 dollars.

B: That's more than I was thinking of giving. Can you sell it for 100 dollars?

A: OK, Let's call it deal.④

B: How much do they come to?

A: 160 dollars.

B: Where can I pay for them?

A: At the cashier's desk over there. By the way, you have to show your passport.

B: Thanks.

3. Buying Clothes 购买衣服

(A: Tourist; B: Tour Leader; C: Clerk)

A: Let's walk on this street. I want to buy a new sweater.

B: Do you want me to come with you?

A: Of course. I want you to look, too. I need your help.

B: Where are we going?

A: Over there, see these sweaters, come with me.

B: There are too many sweaters!

C: Hello. May I help you?

A: Hello. I want to look at a sweater.

C: These sweaters are very beautiful.

A: This is my size.

C: What color do you want?

A: I don't know. Any color.

C: How about the color?

A: Is it too loud for me?[⑤]

B: Yes. It's a bit showy.

A: I like the yellow pants in the window.

C: Oh, yes. It is very nice. Wait a minute, please. I'm going to get them for you.

A: May I try it on?

C: Of course, please!

B: Oh! This sweater shows your figure off nicely.

C: This dress looks nice on you.

A: Yes, it seems to fit well. How much do I owe you?[⑥]

C: It costs 100 dollars.

A: This is nice, but I suppose it's quite expensive.

B: Can you come down a bit?[⑦]

A: I can't give you more than 75 dollars, can you sell it for that?

C: We are practically giving this away.

A: Thank you so much.

C: Not at all, Miss, please come again.

4. Asking For A Refund at a Supermarket 在超市办理退货

(A: Tour Leader; B: Shop Assistant)

Scene 1

A: Excuse me.

B: Yes?

A: A lady in our group bought this digital camera here yesterday. But it doesn't work.

B: Oh, Let's see what's wrong.

A: This button doesn't work. When I push it, nothing happens.

B: You are right. I will give you another one. Do you have the receipt?

A: No, we don't. She left it at the hotel.

B: Sorry. But we can do nothing without the receipt. Come back with it, please.

A: All right. We will go to get it. When will you close?

B: At 5:30 p.m.

A: All right. See you later.

Scene 2

A: Hello, I have come to return this digital camera.

B: Oh, yes. I remember you.

A: Here is the receipt.

B: All right. Let's see if I can find you another one. Oh, here is one. It's a new type. It looks almost the same but it has some more functions.

A: How much is this one?

B: It is 680 dollars.

A: That's more than she paid for the old type.

B: Yes. But for 62 dollars more you'll get more functions.

A: No, thanks. She just wants the type she bought yesterday.

B: I am sorry, but we don't have another one of the old type. This is all we have right now.

A: Do you have a cheaper one?

B: No, this is the cheapest one.

A: In this case she just wants to get her money back.

B: All right. Would you sign here for the refund? We have to keep these records. Here is the refund.

A: Thank you.

5. Tax Refund 办理退税

Scene 1

(A: Salesgirl of a Souvenir Shop; B: Tourist)

A: How about this necklace? It's made of crystal.

B: It looks very nice. How much does it cost?

A: It only costs 480 Euros.

B: I'll take it. Here is 500 Euros.

A: Thank you, sir. Here is your receipt and 20 Euros change.

B: Can I have a fax refund form, please? I'm from China.

A: Certainly, sir. May I have your passport, please? Let me write out a tax refund form for you.

B: By the way, where can we get our tax refund?

A: At any customs of the European Union countries. This is your tax refund form. Please keep it. The 480 Euros you paid includes tax and you can draw it back at the customs with this refund form.

B: Thank you very much, Miss.

A: With pleasure.

Scene 2

(A: Customs Official; B: Tourist; C: Official of the Cash Refund)

A: Good morning, sir. May I help you?

B: Yes. Is this the place where I can draw back the tax paid for the necklace I bought in Austria? I'd like to have my tax refund form stamped.

A: Certainly, sir. May I have your passport, boarding pass, tax refund form, and the merchandise you've bought, please?

B: Here you are.

A: All right. Here is your refund form. Please go to get your tax refund at the Cash Refund Counter at the Emigration.

B: I see. Thank you, officer.

* * *

B: Excuse me, sir. May I get my tax refund here?

C: Certainly, sir. Can I have your stamped refund form, please?

B: Here you are, and my passport and boarding pass.

C: Thank you. You've paid 480 Euros for the necklace. The tax is 17%. So you'll get a refund of 81.6 Euros. How would you like to have it, get it in cash or send it to your credit account?

B: Cash, please.

A: All right. Here are your passport, boarding pass and 81.6 Euros tax refund.

B: Thank you very much.

Notes 注释

① on my word 我敢保证

② rock bottom price 最低价

③ You can't be wrong on that. 这个价你不会吃亏的。

④ Let's call it deal. 成交了。

⑤ Is it too loud for me? 我穿这件衣服是不是太花哨?
   loud having offensively bright colors 过分花哨的

⑥ How much do I owe you? 多少钱?

⑦ Can you come down a bit? 你能略微降点价吗?

Useful Sentences 必学句型

1. Would you like jewelry?
   您要不要首饰?

2. Today is Mother's Day and all the jewelry is on sale at Rich's.
   今天是母亲节,瑞奇店的所有首饰全部打折出售。

3. Do you have gold jewels?
   你们有黄金饰品吗?

4. Yes, we have 14K and 18K gold necklaces, chains and earrings.
   有,我们有14K和18K的金项链、手链和耳环。

5. May I have a look?
   我能看一下吗?

6. Sure. Here is a nice gold necklace.
   当然可以。这里有一根很好的金项链。

7. Its regular price is $56, and now you can have it with a twenty percent discount.
   原价是56美元,现在可以让你打八折买下。

8. It's very elegant. I'll take it.
   这项链非常精致,我买了。

9. I want to buy some jewellery.
   我要买些首饰。

10. What kind of jewellery do you like to have?
    你要哪种首饰呢?

11. I should like to look at some bracelets.
    我想看看手镯。

12. Pure gold or carats?
    纯金的还是K金的?

13. What's the price for this bracelet?
    这只手镯多少钱?

14. How about five hundred dollars?
    500元怎么样?

15. I'm sorry we only sell at fixed price.
    很抱歉,我们店不还价。

16. I wish to buy a diamond ring, too.
    我还想买只钻戒。

17. Is this one suitable for you?
    这只适合你吗?

18. No, it seems too old fashioned to me.
    不,我觉得似乎太老式了。

19. Let me try it on. Oh, it's too small for me, haven't you got any larger ones?
    让我戴戴看,呵,太小了,有稍大点儿的吗?

20. This fits me well, how much do you charge for it?
    这只很合适，多少钱？

21. Is that a real string of pearls?
    那串珍珠是真的吗？

22. You may take it on my word, if you find out it is an imitation you may return it to me.
    请相信我的话，假如您发现是假的可以拿来退还给我。

Passage Reading 阅读材料

National Tax Refund Service

National Tax Refund Service offers all non-resident visitors who come to Canada a convenient and easy way to claim their sales tax refund on the eligible goods and accommodations purchased, while in Canada. National saves you time and money!

National's knowledgeable team is devoted to obtaining the greatest tax refund for their clients. We offer more experience in processing tax refunds for both leisure and business travel, including claims for foreign conventions held in Canada. Our experts handle all paperwork and take care of all the administrative requirements. No calculations are required! You only have to fill out our form and send it along with the receipts for eligible goods and accommodations. National handles everything else.

By using National's service, non-resident visitors to Canada may choose one of two convenient methods to receive their tax refund: cheque in US dollars (US residents only); credited to one of 5 major credit cards: Visa, Master Card, American Express, Diners Club or JCB Card.

Exercises 练习

1. **Reading and Translation**

The longest river in the world, the Nile, flows through the north-western area of Africa, and then into the Mediterranean Sea. Great civilizations have always flourished alongside rivers, but the Egyptian civilization, which started on the Nile, is the most fascinating and mysterious in the history of mankind. The Nile valley is a fertile one where there is an abundance of water and sun, elements which the ancient Egyptian believed were gods, they called the sun Amon and the Nile Apis. Memphis was the first great capital of Egypt, united as a single kingdom in the third millennium B. C.. But the Nile burst its banks a few centuries ago, flooding the ancient capital. The river however has given more than it has taken, enough to make Herodotus, the ancient Greek historian say: Egypt is a gift from the Nile. The annual floods left precious silt on the fields, a miraculous natural fertilizer which made. The crops grow luxuriantly.

2. **Complete the Following Dialogues in English with the hints given in Chinese**

(1) (A: Clerk; B: Miss Yuan)
A: 你想买哪一种珠宝？
B: _____
A: 你要黄金的还是白金的？

B: _____

A: 好的, 小姐。

B: _____

A: 590 美元。

B: _____

A: 这个价格很适中。

B: _____

A: 我们前几天才降价, 这个价格很优惠。

B: _____

A: 哦, 那好吧。

(2)（A: Customer; B: Salesperson）

A: 不好意思, 对于这套衣服请你给点建议吧。

B: _____

A: 你能帮忙改一改吗?

B: _____

A: 这一套多少钱?

B: _____

A: 哦, 我想我付不起, 我还是看看好了。

B: _____

A: 谢谢。

B: _____

3. Role-play

Situation A

One of your tourists bought a camera at the supermarket. However, he found that the lens of the camera had broken when he got to the hotel. Then he went back to that supermarket to ask for a refund at a supermarket. Go with your tourist and help him to get the refund at the supermarket. Make up a dialogue between you and the salesman.

Situation B

You intend to buy some cigarettes and wines at the duty free shop. But you suppose that the price is not reasonable. Now you begin to bargain with the saleswoman.

Unit 8 Free Activities 参与游客自由活动

本课导读

在自由活动阶段，领队有时会和游客一起自由活动。作为领队，要对国外的各种交通方式有所了解，比如地铁，公共汽车和出租车等。领队还要能用英语问路，陪客人看医生和帮助客人邮寄包裹、明信片和信件等。在自由活动中，领队要竭尽所能保护客人的人身安全，不要建议游客去参加危险的活动。

Special Terms 专业词汇

traffic regulation	交通规则	slippery when wet	潮湿路滑
guide post	路标	steep hill	陡坡
milestone	里程碑	rough road	不平的路
mark car stop	停车标志	curve road; bend road	弯路
traffic light	红绿灯	winding road	连续的弯路
automatic traffic signal light	自动红绿灯	double bend road	之字路
red light	红灯	switch back road	之字公路
green light	绿灯	dangerous down grade	下坡危险
amber light	黄灯	road junction	道路交叉点
traffic post	交通岗	cross road	十字路
police box	岗亭	turn left	左转
traffic police	交通警	turn right	右转
pantomime	打手势	keep left	靠左
single line	单行线	keep right	靠右
double white lines	双白线	slow	慢驶
dual carriage-way	双程线	speed	速度
zebra stripes	斑马线	excessive speed	超速
traffic line marker	划路线机	speed limit	速度限制
artery traffic	交通干线	resume speed	恢复速度
carriage-way	车行道	no through traffic	禁止通行
lane auxiliary	辅助车道	blocked	此路不通
two-way traffic	双车道	no entry	不准驶入
cyclists only	自行车通行	keep in line/no overhead	不准超越
one way only	单行道	no turns	不准掉头
narrow road	窄路	passing bay	让车道

Situational Conversations   情景对话

1. Taking Subways   乘地铁

(A: Tourist; B: Policeman)

Scene 1

A: Which line do I take for Greenwich Village?

B: You can take the D, the F or the A. Just make sure you're going downtown.

A: How do I get down to the trains?

B: Take the escalator and then go to the right.

A: What time's the next train?

B: That's 9:26 on Track 16.

A: When does it get there?

B: It's scheduled to arrive at 9:45.

A: How much is it?

B: It's 10 dollars.

Scene 2

A: What track does the train leave from?

B: That's track 1 at 11:15.

A: What time does it get in?

B: It gets in around 11:45.

A: What's the fare?

B: It is 9 dollars.

Scene 3

A: Can I buy a monthly pass[①] for the subway?

B: Yes. You can get a pass from that dispensing machine[②] over there.

A: Thank you. Is there a limit to how many rides you get?

B: There are a couple choices. You can get a 30-ride pass, you can get an unlimited pass, and there is an unlimited weekly pass.

A: Oh, really. Great. Thanks for your help.

B: You are welcome.

2. Taking Taxi   乘出租车

(A: Tourist; B: Taxi Driver)

Scene 1

B: Good morning, where do you intend to go?

A: Grand Central Station, please. I have to be there by 7:00.

B: I think you'll make it[③] if we don't get stuck in a traffic jam.

A: Oh, thanks.

B: Not at all.

A: Pardon, please. How far away is it from the Hilton Hotel to Grand Central Station?

B: It is no distance at all, about five miles away. Here we are. That's $9.15, please.

A: Here is $10. Keep the change.④

Scene 2

A: The Sun Hotel, please. I have to be there by 6:00.

B: We shouldn't have any trouble if the traffic isn't too heavy. Is this your first trip here?

A: Yes, I've never been here before.

B: You haven't seen the sights yet, have you?

A: No, I'm open to suggestion.⑤

B: Why don't you visit the Statue of Liberty first?

A: That's a good idea.

B: Here we are. That will be seven dollars and seventy cents.

A: Thanks a lot. Here's ten dollars. Keep the change.

3. Accompanying the Sick Tourist to the Hospital 陪旅客看医生

(A: Tour Leader; B: Doctor)

Scene 1

A: My friend, Mr. Yu, has a sore throat and his chest hurts.

B: How long has he been like this?

A: Two or three days now.

B: I think he has got the flu. There's a lot of it going around.⑥

A: What do you think he ought to do?

B: Get this prescription filled and go straight to bed.

Scene 2

A: Mr. Song has the chills and an upset stomach.

B: How long has he felt like this?

A: For most of the week.

B: It sounds as if he has a virus.

A: What do you think he should do?

B: I'll give him something. I want him to take it easy and come back in a couple of days.

Scene 3

A: Mr. Fu feels dizzy and he has a headache.

B: How long has he been sick?

A: Since yesterday.

B: He seems to be generally run-down.

A: What can he do?

B: It's nothing serious, but he had better stay in bed for a day or two.⑦

4. Asking the Way to the Mail Office 询问邮局地址

(A: Miss Wang; B: Policeman)

Scene 1

A: Pardon me. I wonder if you could tell me how to get to the mail office.

B: Keep going straight for two blocks, then turn right on Elm Street and you'll run right into it.

A: Is it too far to walk?

B: No. It's only a little way.

A: Thanks.

B: Sure. Have a good day.

Scene 2

A: Can you help me out? I'm trying to find a post office.

B: Go three blocks and make a right. It's right there.

A: Should I take the bus?

B: No. It only takes about five minutes to walk.

A: Thank you very much.

B: Any time.

5. Mailing Letters, Post Cards and Parcels 邮寄信件、明信片和包裹

(A: Tour Leader; B: Clerk)

A: I need stamps to send eight post cards. How much are they?

B: Eight cents each. Anything else?

A: I also need ten fifteen-cent stamps. I want to send this package. Which window should I go to?

B: Go to the window marked "Parcel Post".

A: Thanks.

(At parcel post window)

I want to send this package parcel post, registered.

B: What does it contain?

A: There are books and manuscripts.

B: Do you want it insured?

A: Yes, please, for thirty dollars.

B: That will be forty cents. Here are your stamps.

A: Thanks.

(The tour leader sticks the stamps on the package and gives it to the clerk.)

I also need to buy some aerograms. Which window is for that?

B: Go to window 9. …Wait a second, Miss.

A: Yes?

B: You forgot to put the return address on the package.

A: Oh, sorry. I'll put it on right now.

B: Now, here is your receipt.

A: Thanks. Is everything done?

B: Yes, Miss. You may go to window 9 now.

Notes 注释

① monthly pass   月票

② dispensing machine   自动售票机

③ make it   及时抵达；He finally made it as an actor.   他最后成了一名成功的演员。

④ keep the change   不用找零钱了

⑤ I'm open to suggestion.   我愿意听听你的意见。

⑥ going around to pass from one person to another; circulate   四处传播

⑦ It's nothing serious, but he had better stay in bed for a day or two.   这不严重，但他最好在床上休息一两天。

Useful Sentences   必学句型

1. Excuse me, can you tell me the way to the post office?
   劳驾，能告诉我去邮局怎么走吗？

2. Go down this road until you come to the traffic lights, and you'll find it.
   沿着这条路走到红绿灯处，你就会看见了。

3. How much more do we have to pay for the express?
   那么坐快车的话，我们要多付多少钱？

4. Then give me two second-class tickets on the express, please.
   那么来两张二等快车票。

5. We are going to the East Village. Which train should we take?
   我们要去东方村庄该坐哪一列车呢？

6. How long will I have to wait?
   我要等多久？

7. According to the kilometer rage, the first 5 kilometers are 4 dollars and every kilometer extra costs you 50 cents.
   我们按千米计算里程，前5千米起价4美元，每超过1千米加收50美分。

8. How much do I owe you?
   车费是多少？

9. I think we'll get there if there are no delays on the way.
   我想如果路上不耽搁，我们可以到达那里。

10. How exactly do you figure out the car fare?
    你们的车费怎么计算？

11. Take the uptown A train and get off at the next station.
    坐往北去的A线车，坐一站就下。

12. Do you want it insured?
    你想给它上保险吗?

  Passage Reading   阅读材料

Safe Eats and Drinks

So what foods are safe to eat? Any foods that have been boiled are generally safe, as well as fruits and vegetables that have to be peeled before eating. Avoid eating uncooked or undercooked meat or meat that is not cooked just prior to serving.

Stay away from foods that require a lot of handling before serving. Here's an example: Nine friends ate at a restaurant when on a school trip overseas; eight had diarrhea the next day. The one who didn't get sick was the only one who had ordered a dish that didn't need to be touched by human hands right before serving.

One of your favorite foods at home is on the safe list on the road—pizza! Pizza dough, sauce, and cheese are foods that are less likely to spoil than others, and the high heat of a pizza oven tends to kill any harmful bacteria in the food.

You've probably heard that you shouldn't drink the water in some countries overseas, but do you know why? Water supplies in many developing countries are not treated in the same way as water supplies in developed countries; various bacteria, viruses, and parasites are commonly found in the water. Many experts suggest you drink only bottled water when traveling. If you need to use tap water, you should boil it first or purify it with an iodine tablet. Even if you're brushing your teeth, rinsing contact lenses, drinking a small glass of water to wash down pills, or adding ice to your drink, first take precautions to ensure the water is safe.

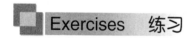 **Exercises   练习**

1. **Reading and Translation**

Wachau is a region that is famous for the presence of vast holdings of fertile vines. This is the most luxuriant and picturesque valley along the entire course of the Danube, where the oblique rays of the sun on the orchards create this typical landscape that traditional iconography would associate with an earthly paradise.

The fruit that grows best in this valley is without a doubt the grape, which is picked in order to be crushed and pressed and transformed into top quality wine. In Krems, a town in the Wachau valley, we find a wine cellar where you can taste full 140 different types of Austrian wine.

The water of the Danubes evokes imagination at every curve, touching on dreamlike places. It continues on its way. The Danube is flowing to the east towards modern Europe, towards a world that renew itself with a new dawn.

2. **Complete the Following Dialogues in English with the hints given in Chinese**

(1) (A: Guest; B: Taxi Driver)

A: _____

B: 如果交通不太拥挤的话,应该是没问题。你是第一次到这吧?

A：_____

B：你还没有看这里的风景吧？

A：_____

B：为什么不先看看自由女神像？

A：_____

B：我们到了。车费是 7 美元 70 美分。

A：_____

(2)（A：Tourist；B：Policeman）

A：_____

B：不，它不到。去国家历史博物馆没有直达的公交车。

A：_____

B：你可在 24 大街转车。

A：_____

B：哦，从这只有三个站。

A：_____

B：不客气。

3. **Role-Play**

Situation A

You are a tour leader. You want to go with your tourists to Fashion department store for shopping. You decide to go there by subway. However, you don't know how to get there. Therefore, you ask a local resident for help. Make up a dialogue between you and the local resident.

Situation B

You are a tour leader. A guest asks you to send post cards back home for him. You go to the post office to send the mail for her, although you are not familiar with the city.

Unit 9 Cooperating with the Local Guide 配合地陪工作

本课导读

和地陪进行有效的沟通，配合地陪工作是领队最重要的职责之一。到达目的机场时，领队首先要尽快根据自己所掌握的信息联络上地陪，并且与对方核对行程。如有出入，应及时与地陪商榷，并告知游客最终的行程安排。若在途中遇到突发事件，如游客走失、饭菜质量问题，领队要沉着冷静，并与地陪商量解决。

Special Terms 专业词汇

late snack	宵夜	artificial color	人工色素
dinner	正餐	distilled water	蒸馏水
ham and egg	火腿肠	long-life milk	保鲜奶
buttered toast	奶油土司	condensed milk	炼乳；炼奶
French toast	法国土司	coffee mate	奶精
muffin	松饼	coffee	咖啡
cheese cake	酪饼	iced coffee	冰咖啡
brown bread	黑面包	white coffee	牛奶咖啡
French roll	小型法式面包	black coffee	纯咖啡
appetizer	开胃菜	ice-cream cone	甜筒
green salad	蔬菜沙拉	vanilla ice-cream	香草冰淇淋
onion soup	洋葱汤	milk-shake	奶昔
potage	法国浓汤	straw	吸管
corn soup	玉米浓汤	French cuisine	法国菜
minestrone	蔬菜面条汤	today's special	今日特餐
ox tail soup	牛尾汤	chef's special	主厨特餐
fried chicken	炸鸡	buffet	自助餐
roast chicken	烤鸡	specialty	招牌菜
T-bone steak	T骨牛排	continental cuisine	欧式西餐
filet steak	菲力牛排	aperitif	饭前酒
sirloin steak	沙朗牛排	dim sum	点心
club steak	小牛排	French fires	炸薯条
chlorella	绿藻	baked potato	烘马铃薯
soda water	苏打水	mashed potatoes	马铃薯泥

Unit 9　Cooperating with the Local Guide　配合地陪工作

pastries	甜点	sunny side up	煎一面荷包蛋
pickled vegetables	泡菜	over-sides	煎两面荷包蛋
crab meat	蟹肉	fried egg	煎蛋
conch	海螺	scramble eggs	炒蛋
escargots	田螺	boiled egg	煮蛋
braised beef	炖牛肉	roast meat	铁板烤肉
bacon	熏肉	sashimi	生鱼片
poached egg	荷包蛋	butter	奶油

Situational Conversations　情景对话

1. Meeting the Local Guide　联络地陪

(A: Tour Leader; B: Local Guide)

A: Are you Mr. Johnson, our local guide from United Travel Service?

B: Yes, You must be the tour leader from CTS.① Welcome to Australia! Glad to meet you, Miss…?

A: I am Grace Lou. Glad to meet you, Mr. Johnson!

B: Me, too! Where are your group members?

A: They are coming. We have got 25 tourists all together in our group.

B: OK. We have arranged 13 standard rooms for your group which enjoys a high reputation② in our beautiful country.

A: It sounds good.

B: Have all got their belongings?

A: Let me see. Yes, they have.

B: Shall we take them to the bus?

A: Certainly. Show us to our bus, please.

B: Ladies and gentlemen, please follow me to the bus!

2. Discussing the Tour Arrangement　商谈旅游行程安排

(A: Tour Leader; B: Local Guide)

A: Everything is OK. Let's discuss the itinerary, Mr. Johnson.

B: OK. Do you have any suggestions in mind?

A: I believe you know your country better. Because this is a young group, I wish you can make the best of the time and try to let them see as many places as possible.

B: Don't worry about that. Our itinerary covers almost all the famous tourist attractions③ in Australia.

A: How long will we stay in Sydney?

B: We will stay for two nights in Sydney. As one of the most beautiful cities in the world,

Sydney has a stunning harbor and beaches, exciting shopping and eating centers, and a great nightlife scene.

A: That is terrific. Don't spend too much time in shopping because they don't like it.

B: I see.

A: Could you give them more time for the harbor and beaches?

B: Certainly.

A: Thank you for your consideration!

B: Wish we had a perfect cooperation.

3. Looking For the Missing Tourist 寻找走失游客

(A: Tour Leader; B: Local Guide)

A: Is everybody on the bus?

B: No, Mrs. Tang, the old woman isn't here.

A: Do you know where she is?

B: I have no idea. Ten minutes ago, I saw her walking around in a souvenir store.

A: She must have lost her way.

B: We have to find her now.

A: You had better take our group to the next stop. I will try to look for her.

B: OK, if you encounter some problems, please let me know.

A: Could you repeat your mobile phone number?

B: My phone number is 93052345.

A: When I find her, I will inform you immediately.

B: Keep in touch.

A: Sure. Take good care of our group members.

……

A: Hello, This is Sandy speaking. I have already found Mrs. Tang.

B: Wonderful news! Where are you?

A: We are now on the Lincool Street. What about your next stop?

B: Our next stop is the Sydney Opera House.

A: How can we get to the Sydney Opera House?

B: You can go north along the street and take Bus 5 to Sydney Opera. You can't miss it.④

A: Pardon, which bus shall we take?

A: Bus 5.

B: OK, I have got it. We will catch up with you as soon as possible.

A: That is quite good. See you then.

B: See you.

4. Negotiating About the Quality of the Meal 交涉饭菜质量问题

(A: Tour Leader; B: Local Guide; C: Manger)

A: The steak has already gone bad. We can not eat the food of that quality.

B: Oh, sorry. I will ask the waiter to change it.

A: My guest wants to get compensation for it.

B: I will ask the manager of the restaurant to talk to you.

C: I am awfully sorry for inconvenience caused.⑤ This steak will be free of charge and one more free salad will be offered.

A: That sounds reasonable.

C: The things like this will not happen again.

A: To be frank, your service is quite good.

C: Thank you. Enjoy your meal, please.

A: See you.

C: Goodbye.

5. Negotiating About the Change of the Itinerary 交涉改变旅游行程

(A: Tour Leader; B: Local Guide)

A: Mr. Johnson, it seems that the itinerary is not suitable for the old tourists.

B: Shall everything be slow and relaxing?

A: Certainly, they want to have a relaxing holiday.

B: I will set the morning call at 8:30.

A: That will be nice.

B: If we get up late, we will probably have no time to enjoy some places in the itinerary.

A: Don't worry about that. They come here for the second time.

B: That is to say, we do not have to go some regular scenic spots.

A: Not exactly, they have already given me a list of tourist attractions.

B: OK, Let me see.

A: Can you put all the places into our new itinerary?

B: It is not a difficult job for me.

A: Terrific! They will appreciate it if you can meet their long desires.

B: It's my pleasure. Don't hesitate to get in touch with me, if you run into problems.

A: Sure.

Notes 注释

① CTS: China Travel Service 中国旅行社

② enjoys a high reputation 享有盛誉

③ tourist attractions 游览胜地

④ You can't miss it. 你一定会找得到的。

⑤ I am awfully sorry for inconvenience caused. 给您带来麻烦,我非常抱歉。

Useful Sentences　必学句型

1. I've come to make sure that your stay in Beijing is a pleasant one.
   我特地为你们安排的，希望你们在北京玩得愉快。
2. You're going out of your way for us, I believe.
   我相信这是对我们的特殊照顾了。
3. It's just the matter of the schedule, that is, if it is convenient for you right now.
   如果你们感到方便的话，我想现在讨论一下日程安排的问题。
4. I think we can draw up a tentative plan now.
   我认为现在可以先草拟一个临时方案。
5. If he wants to make some changes, minor alternations can be made then.
   如果他有什么意见的话，我们还可以对计划稍加修改。
6. So our evenings will be quite full then?
   那么我们的活动在晚上也安排满了吗？
7. We'll leave some evenings free, that is, if it is all right with you.
   如果你们愿意的话，我们想留几个晚上供你们自由支配。
8. I can't say for certain off-hand.
   我还不能马上说定。
9. We've arranged our schedule without any trouble.
   我们已经很顺利地把活动日程安排好了。
10. Here is a copy of itinerary I have worked out for you and your guests. Would you please have a look at it?
    这是我为客人拟定的活动日程安排。请过目一下，好吗？
11. If you have any questions on the details, feel free to ask.
    如果对某些细节有意见的话，请提出来。
12. I can see you have put a lot of time into it.
    我相信你在制订这个计划上一定花了不少精力吧。
13. We really wish you'll have a pleasant stay here.
    我们真诚地希望你们在这里过得愉快。
14. I wonder if it is possible to arrange shopping for us.
    我想能否在我们访问结束时为我们安排一点时间购物。

Passage Reading　阅读材料

Stopping the Gush

Try these simple tips to stop your nosebleed:

- Get some tissues or a damp cloth to catch the blood.
- Sit or stand so your head is above your heart.
- Tilt your head forward and pinch your nostrils together just below the bony center part of your nose. Applying pressure helps stop the blood flow and the nosebleed will usually stop with 10

full minutes of steady pressure——don't keep checking to see if the bleeding has stopped.

Apply a cold compress, such as ice wrapped in a cloth or paper towel, to the area around the nose. Applying pressure with a cotton pad inside the upper lip may also help.

If you get a nosebleed, don't blow your nose. Doing so can cause additional nosebleeds. Also, don't tilt your head back. This common practice will cause blood to run into your throat. If you swallow the blood, you might throw up.

If you've tried the steps above twice and the bleeding continues after 10 minutes, you'll need to see your school nurse or your doctor.

Once you've stopped the initial nosebleed, don't lift heavy objects or do other activities that cause you to strain, and don't blow your nose for 24 hours. Also, keep your head elevated above your heart.

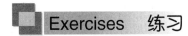

Exercises 练习

1. Reading and Translation

Language is an important part of culture. Learning a foreign language includes learning a new culture. It should be a fun and interesting process. However, traditional Chinese English teaching is basically grammar and knowledge centered. And teachers have tended to pay too much attention to the correctness of English. Therefore, many students lost their interest in learning English. They may get good marks in tests but their ability to use English, especially their listening and talking skills tend not to be adequate.

To solve this problem, Chinese English teaching experts and officials from the Education Department have established a series of reforms in the teaching of English in primary and high schools. One of the reforms allows the local education department to choose their own textbooks based upon the national teaching guideline.

2. Complete the Following Dialogues in English with the hints given in Chinese

(1) (A: Tour Leader; B: Local Guide)
A: 布莱克先生, 这个行程不适合老年人。
B: _____
A: 是的, 他们想过一个轻松的假期。
B: _____
A: 那对他们来说太早。
B: _____
A: 比较合理。
B: _____
A: 别担心, 他们给了我一份想去的景点清单。
B: _____
A: 你能把景点都纳入行程吗?
B: _____
A: 太好啦! 假如你能满足他们的要求, 他们肯定很感激你。

B：_____

A：好的。

（2）（A：Tour Leader；B：Local Guide）

A：对不起，是约翰逊先生吗？

B：_____

A：我是来自浙江中国旅行社的托尼。

B：_____

A：很高兴见到你，弗兰克！

B：_____

C：很高兴见到你，托尼！欢迎来美国。

A：_____.

C：很荣幸，希望你们旅途愉快。

A：_____

C：这是你第二次来美国吗，托尼？

A：_____

C：希望你们在美国玩得愉快。

A：_____

B：所有游客都到了吗？

A：_____

B：车在停车场，我们走吧。

3. Role-Play

Situation A

You are a tour leader. The restaurant served the bad milk which made people feel bad. The guests want to get some compensation from the restaurant. You talk to the restaurant manager about the compensation issues. Make up a dialogue between you and the restaurant manager.

Situation B

You are a tour leader. Guests intend to enjoy as many places as possible, but the itinerary is not proper for them. On behalf of the guests, you are negotiating with the local guide about the arrangements.

Part III

Key to the exercises
练习答案

Part I Inbound Tourism
入境旅游

 Unit 1

1. Reading and Translation

女士们,先生们:

下午好!

欢迎大家来到上海。请大家安心坐好,不用去担心你们的行李。我们有另外的车将它们直接送到你们下榻的酒店。

首先请允许我作个自我介绍。我们的司机姓张。张师傅已有20年的驾龄,所以大家坐他的车是绝对安全的。我的名字叫郭强。我们是上海国际旅行社的。在此我代表我们旅行社及我的同事对你们的到来表示热烈的欢迎。

你们在上海期间,我和张师傅将竭诚为你们服务。我们将尽最大的努力使大家的上海之行成为一次愉快的经历。如果大家有什么困难或问题,请尽管告诉我们,不要犹豫。

预祝大家在上海玩得开心。

2. Complete the Following Dialogues in English with the hints given in Chinese

(1)

A: Excuse me, but aren't you Mr. Smith?

B: Yes, I am.

A: I am Wang Yongjun from Zhejiang CITS.

B: How do you do, Mr. Wang?

A: How do you do? Our manager, Mr. Lin has come to meet you. May I introduce him to you? This is our manager, Mr. Lin. This is Mr. Smith from American Pacific Delight.

C: How do you do, Mr. Smith? Welcome to Hangzhou.

B: How do you do? It's very kind of you to come to meet us.

C: Oh, it is a pleasure. I hope you have had a pleasant trip.

B: Very nice. Thank you.

C: Is this your first time to Hangzhou, Mr. Smith?

B: Yes, the very first.

C: Hope you will have a good time here in Hangzhou.

B: Thank you. I am sure we will.

A: All the tourists are here. The coach is waiting in the park. Let's go.

(2)

B: No, I am afraid you have made a mistake.

A: I'm so sorry.

B: Never mind.

C: Oh, I'm a member of the tour group from America. Mr. Brown is our tour leader. He is over there.

A: Excuse me, but aren't you Mr. Brown from the United States?

D: Why, yes.

A: How do you do, Mr. Brown? Welcome to Hangzhou. I am the guide from China Youth Travel Service. My name is Liu Wei.

D: How do you do, Mr. Liu? Nice to meet you. Thank you for coming to meet us.

A: Did you enjoy you trip, Mr. Brown?

D: Yes, we had a very pleasant trip.

A: Is everybody here now?

D: Let me see. Yes, everyone is here.

A: Our bus is waiting outside in the park. Let's go.

Unit 2

1. Reading and Translation

秦始皇兵马俑博物馆

1974年3月，几个村民在秦始皇陵东1.5千米处打井时，意外发现了许多碎陶人，经考古工作者探测，这里是一个长方形的秦代兵马俑坑。1976年通过钻探，在这个坑的北侧20米和25米处又发现两处兵马俑坑。按照它们被发现的时间先后考古工作者把它们分别定名为兵马俑一号坑、二号坑和三号坑。三个坑的总面积为22 780平方米。

这一发现震惊中外。为了妥善保护这些罕见的、具有重要历史价值的文物，国务院于1975年批准在原址上建造博物馆，于1979年国庆节正式对外开放。秦始皇兵马俑博物馆作为中国十大名胜之一，于1987年被联合国教科文组织列为世界文化遗产。

2. Complete the Following Dialogues in English with the hints given in Chinese

(1)

A: Good evening. May I help you, sir?

B: My guest Mr. Tom Jordan booked one double room and one twin room two weeks ago.

A: How do you spell his last name, please?

B: J-O-R-D-A-N, Jordan.

A: Thank you. Just a moment, please. I will check the arrival list…Yes, we have his reservation. A double room for Mr. and Mrs. Jordan and a twin room for Betty and Mary. Is that right?

B: That is right.

A: Would you please ask his to fill in this registration form?

B: Yes, of course.

A: May I confirm your departure date, Mr. Jordan?

C: It is on the 9th.

A: How would you like to make your payment?

C: By credit card.

A: May I take a print of your card now, please?

C: Here you are.

A: Thank you.

(2)

B: Good afternoon. I would like to have a room.

A: Good afternoon, sir. Single or double?

B: Single, please.

A: Have you made a reservation?

B: I sent you an e-mail last week from Beijing, but I didn't receive an answer.

A: May I know your name, please?

B: The name is Taylor.

A: Yes, we've received your e-mail. And we are holding a room for Mr. Taylor.

B: That's great. How much for a night?

A: It's 240 yuan per night.

B: Mr. Taylor, the room rate is 240 yuan. How do you like it?

C: All right. Let's take it.

A: How long do you plan to stay, Mr. Taylor?

C: Until Wednesday. I'll check out on Wednesday morning.

A: Would you please fill in the registration form, Mr. Taylor? I'll get a bellboy to take your bags and show you to your room.

C: Thank you very much.

Unit 3

1. Reading and Translation

九点钟我们离开了酒店，这天也一直下着雨。尽管如此，整个团队的情绪仍然很高涨。上午我们参观了中山纪念堂、陈家祠、南越王墓，下午我们去游玩了沙面岛。

这是旅行的最后一天，因此许多客人想去买东西。吴小姐带我们去了环市东路的友谊商店。那是个购物的好地方，在那里，可以买到中国丝绸、服装、珠宝、手工艺品、古董、佛山剪纸、瓷器和漆器等。客人们对这个商场的物品太感兴趣了，我们不得不将原定五点半的晚餐推迟到七点半。晚餐的时候，派克夫人评论说：广州保持了它独特的与其他中国城市不同的文化传统，包括其世界闻名的、我们大家都喜欢的美味佳肴。

2. Complete the Following Dialogues in English with the hints given in Chinese

(1)

B: It seems everything is settled. Shall we have a discussion on the itinerary, Mr. Wang?

A: Oh, yes. Have you got anything special in mind that you would like to see?

B: I think you know your city better than I do. But this is an old group. Everything has to be slow and relaxing.

A: I see. So in the morning, we will leave the hotel at 9:00 for the cruise on the West Lake.

B: At what time does the boat leave?

A: Ten thirty.

B: Why do we leave so much earlier?

A: We will visit a park before we take the boat.

B: I see. But do we have to do that?

A: No. We can drive pretty close to the dock.

B: Can we do that and leave the hotel later?

A: No problem if you like. We can put our departure off to a quarter to ten in that case.

B: That sounds perfect.

(2)

A: Good morning!

B: Good morning.

A: Can I help you?

B: My wife and I want to see the places of interest in Hangzhou. Can you arrange a tour for us?

A: How much time do you have?

B: Two days, tomorrow and the day after tomorrow.

A: The first day, you may take the north routine while the second, the south.

B: what are the attractions?

A: The north routine includes Lingyin Temple, General Yuefei's Tomb and Temple, cruise on the West Lake, the south routine covers the Tiger Spring Park, Six Harmonies Pagoda and the Meijiawu Tea Plantation.

B: It sounds nice. How much do they cost?

A: 700 yuan per person.

B: Besides the park entrance fee, what else is covered?

A: Besides the park entrance fee, it also includes a private car and guide for two days and two lunches.

B: The price sounds reasonable. We will take it. Shall we pay for it now or…

A: You may pay for it now or do it after finishing the itinerary.

B: Thank you. Can you let the guide pick us up at 9:00 at Wanghu Hotel tomorrow morning?

A: Yes of course. Would you please leave us your room number?

B: Sure. It's 218.

A: The guide will surely come to pick you up tomorrow morning. See you.

B: Thank you. Bye-bye.

Unit 4

1. Reading and Translation

常言道"上有天堂，下有苏杭"。早在13世纪时，马可波罗来到杭州，他将杭州称为"世界上最美丽、最华贵的城市，……在这里人们有如此多的享乐，以至于他们想象他们是在天堂里生活"。

西湖是这个城市美景的焦点。她的宽为三英里，周围九英里。这里有小岛、寺庙、古亭、园林、长堤、拱桥和花草树木。所有这些使得杭州西湖"风景如画"。

西湖被白堤和苏堤分成三个部分。这两条长堤景色优美，充满诗情画意，已成为西湖上人们理想的散步之地。白堤是根据白居易的名字命名的。白居易是唐朝著名的诗人，因失宠于朝廷而在公元 822 年到 824 年间被贬为杭州刺史。期间他让人们用湖里挖出的淤泥堆成了这条堤。

2. Complete the Following Dialogues in English with the hints given in Chinese

（1）

A：Good morning, sir.

B：Good morning. It is a lovely day today, isn't it?

A：Yes. It's a wonderful day for touring.

B：So where are you going to take us today?

A：I'll show you first of all to a famous ancient pagoda. It's called Six Harmonies Pagoda.

B：Six Harmonies Pagoda?

A：An interesting name, isn't it? I'll tell you why later.

B：All right. What else are we going to do?

A：We will also visit a tea plantation.

B：That sounds interesting, too.

A：I'm sure you will enjoy them.

（2）

A：Good morning, sir.

B：Good morning. You said we were going to have a boat ride on the lake, didn't you?

A：Yes, our first program is the lake cruise.

B：How great!

A：Now we will start our lake cruise soon. As I told you yesterday that this lake was a lagoon in the past.

B：But now it is such a scenic lake.

A：Yes. Let's enjoy the scenery of the lake together.

B：What is the mound under the pavilion there?

A：That's the tomb of an ancient geisha, Su Xiaoxiao, who has become the symbol of true love now.

B：What a beautiful arched bridge that is next to it!

A：It's called Xiling Bridge, one of the three famous bridges by the lake.

B：Is that causeway the Bai Causeway as you mentioned?

A：No. That is the Su Causeway, which was built under the leadership of another great poet, Su Dongpo.

B：Now we can see the islets in the lake. There are several!

A：Yes, there are three. The largest one, also the most famous one is known as Lesser Fairy Island.

Unit 5

1. Reading and Translation

筷子的使用在我国已有几千年的历史。它既可以用来夹食物，也可以用来将食物从盘/碗里扒进嘴里。除了喝汤或吃冰淇淋，吃其他所有东西都可用它。在中国通常是使用筷子的，但是，如果你担心自己用中国筷子会使你尴尬的话，你完全可以要求用刀或叉。然而，如果你想学学如何使用筷子，你的主人毫无疑问会以极大的耐心来帮助你。随着时间的推移，你会吃惊于你快速的进步。

2. Complete the Following Dialogues in English with the hints given in Chinese

（1）

A：Good evening. Welcome to our restaurant.

B：Good afternoon. Two of my American friends want to taste the specialties of your restaurant.

A：Do you have a reservation?

B：No, I'm afraid not. Do you have a table for two?

A：I'm sorry. There is not table available just now. Would you please wait for a while? The table over there is almost ready.

B：Do you mind waiting for a moment?

C：No. Not at all.

A：The table over there is ready now. Please follow me.

B：Thank you.

（2）

A：Good morning, sir. How many are there of you?

B：Just two of them, please.

A：Which tea do you prefer? We have oolong tea, chrysanthemum tea and green tea.

B：What do you think? I suggest you have green tea.

C：OK. We will have green tea.

A：What would you like to eat? We have various kind of "dim sum".

C：Well, we have no idea of the food here. Can you recommend some to us?

B：With pleasure.

C：Thanks.

B：Miss, may I have the bill, please?

A：OK. It's sixty-eight yuan in total.

C：Here is a hundred.

A：Here is your change. Thirty-two yuan. Thank you for your coming. Welcome again.

Unit 6

1. Reading and Translation

加拿大有繁华的都市，它们体现了这个国家的富裕和现代化的程度，同时也反映着那些来自旧世纪的征服者在短短的几个世纪里开垦这片北美洲的寒冷荒原所取得的辉煌成就。

尽管一代又一代的定居者已经改变了这一片土地的面貌，创造出了现代化的综合设施体系，但加拿大仍然是一个未遭破坏、未遭侵犯的自然世界，大自然仍是这里的主宰。

和地球的任何地方相比，这里的大自然更能让人类惊奇、困惑、着迷，连那些信奉"技术治国论"的人也不例外。在加拿大，自然的力量甚至能创造出一种反自然的力量来。比如，河水能倒流，一直流向源头。

这种反常的现象叫"逆潮"。其原因被归结为大自然产生的一种强大吸引力，正是这种在太阳和月亮的共同作用下形成的引力产生了"潮水"。

2. Complete the Following Dialogues in English with the hints given in Chinese

（1）

A: Are you being served, sir?

B: I'd like to buy a medium-sized cloisonné vase with a light blue background.

A: I'm sorry, sir. They are sold out. We only have some big ones now, but we are expecting to have some tomorrow.

B: Oh, I am leaving China tomorrow. I don't think I have much time.

A: Could you go to the Shanghai Friendship Store and get it there?

B: Let me see. How much is the big one?

A: One hundred and eighty yuan.

B: That sounds reasonable. Will you show me some?

A: Yes, sir. How would you like this one? The background is pale blue with traditional Chinese paintings of flowers and birds.

B: It's attractive. I'll take a pair. I am sure my wife will like them.

A: Yes. I'm sure she will, sir.

B: Can you pack the vases and send them to New York by mail for me?

A: Yes, sir. Please write your name and address on this slip.

B: OK. How much should I pay then?

A: Four hundred yuan altogether, including the postage and the charge for the packing. You know, we'll have to make a special box.

B: All right. Here's the money.

（2）

A: Can I help you, madam?

B: Yes. I'd like to buy some presents for my friends.

A: Would you like jewelry? Today is Mother's Day and all the jewelry is on sale at Rich's.

B: That's great. Do you have gold jewels?

A: Yes, we have 14K and 18K gold necklaces, chain and ear-rings.

B: May I have a look?

A: Sure. Here is nice gold necklace. Its regular price is $56, and now you can have it with a twenty percent discount.

B: It's very elegant. I'll take it.

A: All right. Is there anything else you want?

B: Will you show the that key ring?

A: Yes. Here you are.

B: It's very nice. Give me ten like this. I'm sure they will be good gifts for my friends in Canada.

Unit 7

1. Reading and Translation

随着饮茶的普及，饮茶的方式也开始多样化。在唐朝以前，人们喝茶并不挑剔。他们喝茶是为了解渴或医疗目的。到了唐朝，人们开始讲究茶道，喝茶的过程也似乎很复杂，在准备阶段就得经过好几个步骤。

到了宋朝，人们饮茶比唐朝更精致。唐朝时，喝茶只是在皇家盛行，而宋朝在有些城市出现了茶馆，老百姓也可以去那里喝茶。

明朝的时候，人们主要喝绿茶。花茶在那时也出现了。

现在，人们去茶馆喝茶并不是真的口渴了。退了休的人去茶馆，在那儿聊天，一坐就是一整天。有时人们也在茶馆招待客人。他们一边聊天一边喝茶或吃着零食、点心。

中国人喜欢喝茶，就像西方人喜欢喝咖啡一样。茶叶原产于中国，它成为中国人日常生活的一部分，至少已有1500年的历史。中国的茶馆就如同法国的咖啡馆和英国的酒吧。虽然近来在中国的城市里咖啡馆和酒吧越来越多，但茶馆没有被取代的危险。

2. Complete the Following Dialogues in English with the hints given in Chinese

(1)

A: Are we ready to go?

B: After visiting the Lingyin Temple, we are a bit tired. What are we going to see next?

A: We are going to visit a tea plantation, where you don't have to walk much. We can have a rest while tasting some tea.

B: That's great! I'm thirsty! What kind of tea are we going to drink?

A: Dragon Well, a famous green tea.

B: I've never tasted any green tea. How is green tea different from black tea? I have drunk black tea before.

A: Green tea is lighter than black tea. It's a tea not fermented.

B: Fermented? Could you give us some details?

A: Yes. Black tea is totally fermented. Oolong tea is half fermented, while Dragon Well tea is green tea, which is not fermented.

B: I see. Thank you very much.

A: You are welcome.

(2)

A: Ladies and gentlemen, attention, please. Now we are in the tea garden.

B: How fresh the air here is!

A: Yes. Look around yourselves, it is all green. How can it not be!

B: Are these tea bushes ready for picking?

A: Yes. Do you know which part is picked for drinking?

B: No. We have no idea.

A: Only those tender shoots are picked. Therefore, spring is the beginning of harvesting.

B: How long is the harvesting season in a year?

A: They are picked in spring, summer and autumn. But the tea picked in spring is the best.

B: So the tea picked now is the best, am I right?

A: Yes. You are very right.

B: Can we have a taste of the best tea in a year?

A: Of course. Let's go in.

Unit 8

1. Reading and Translation

紧接着发生的是那些成熟了的蚕从嘴里一圈圈绕着自己吐出的很长的、有黏性的丝。开始的时候，你可以透过一层薄丝看到里面的蚕。当吐丝完了以后茧也就织成了，而蚕也就被裹在里边看不见了。

茧织好以后，蚕农们就把它们捡到竹筐里，然后把它们运到丝绸公司，公司就设在当地农村的收购中心。在收购中心，所有这些茧必须及时进行烘烤，将里面的蛹杀死或闷死。要不这样的话，茧里面的蚕就会由蛹变成蛾跑出蚕茧，使得蚕茧上出现一个窟窿而不能进行缫丝。

2. Complete the Following Dialogues in English with the hints given in Chinese

(1)

A: So, these are the cocoons, aren't they?

B: Yes, they are.

A: What are the workers doing here?

B: They are sorting out the bad ones.

A: Which are the bad ones?

B: Look carefully. You can see not all the cocoons are in good quality. Some are pierced, some are crushed, some have yellow secretion on the surface and some are twin pupae cocoons.

B: I see. So those are the ones to be picked out?

A: Yes, because otherwise the quality of the silk would be degraded.

B: How interesting! Where do the cocoons go from here?

A: They go to the reeling process.

B: Are we going to see that?

A: Yes, let's go now.

(2)

A: Good afternoon, Madame. Welcome to our store. Can I help you?

B: I'm looking for a silk shirt for my husband. Can you show me some, please?

A: Certainly. We have a wide selection of silk shirts here. But what size, please?

B: Large.

A: How do you like these?

B: How nice! They all look beautiful. But the problem is that I'm not good at choosing. I wonder if you could help me.

A: Yes, with pleasure. I would recommend the purple one. It is the fashionable color this year.

B: Thank you. I think this will fit my husband well. How much is it?

A: It's 250 yuan.

B: Can I have a better price?

A: I'm sorry, Madame. Our prices are fixed.

B: OK. I'll take this one. Here is 200 yuan.

A: Here is your change. Thank you.

B: Thank you. Goodbye.

Unit 9

1. Reading and Translation

春　节

中国最重要的节日是春节，也就是中国的新年。春节对于中国人来说就像圣诞节对于西方人一样重要。节日的具体日期由农历而不是公历决定，所以春节的节庆日期在元月下旬与二月上旬之间变化。

新年的准备活动从农历年底开始。人们开始忙活大扫除、清还债务、理发、购买新衣等。家家户户的门上都贴上春联。人们会在家中或去庙里烧香祭祖，祈求老天爷保佑平安。

除夕夜，一家老小团聚在一起吃年夜饭。北方人喜欢吃饺子，而南方人喜欢吃年糕。午夜，人们开始燃放鞭炮以驱赶邪恶，迎接新年。那一时刻，全城上下都淹没在震耳欲聋的爆竹声中。

2. Complete the Following Dialogues in English with the hints given in Chinese

(1)

B: Excuse me. Are you our guide?

A: Yes, I am. Are you Mr. Smith from the United States?

B: Yes. We've been waiting here for more than half an hour! Why are you so late?

A: I'm terribly sorry. Our bus got stuck in a traffic jam.

B: You should have known the traffic is heavy in this hour. Why didn't you start earlier?

A: We did start earlier than usual. But there was an accident which caused a big jam and held us for almost an hour.

B: All right. Now let's not let the guests wait any longer.

A: Right. I'll explain the situation to the guests myself on the bus.

(2)

A: This is the manager of the restaurant, sir.

B: What can I do for you, sir?

C: Are you the manager here? We have to complain about your food. There was a fly in the fish! Look!

B: Yes, I'm the manager. I'm very sorry to have spoilt your evening. Please have this croaker instead.

C: But I'm afraid we haven't ordered this dish.

A: I have negotiated with the manager. There will be no charge for this. This is the compensation for the trouble they caused to you.

B: Please do accept our apologies and be assured that we'll do our best to improve.

C: All right. But we hope it won't happen again.

B: Thank you very much. I hope you will come here again and we'll give you an excellent service as well.

C: Certainly, we will.

B: Have a good trip, my friends.

C: Thanks. We will!

Part II Outbound Tourism
出境旅游

Unit 1

1. Reading and Translation

自由女神像

自由女神像是矗立在纽约湾的一尊巨大塑像。这是法国为纪念美利坚合众国诞生及为延续两国人民的友谊而赠送给美国人民的礼物。

塑像本身的造价大约是 25 万美元，这笔款项由法国筹集，而塑像底座的造价大约是 35 万美元，由美国出资。

塑像本身——一个女子的形象——重 225 吨，高 46 米，底座 93 米。这名女子右手持火炬，左手怀抱一本书，象征美国的《独立宣言》。塑像的眼睛宽 0.79 米，在她的头部可以容纳 40 人。塑像头部的观景台高出海平面 79 米，在那里人们可以观赏纽约湾的美景，特别是在晚上，火炬还会发出橘黄色的光。

这尊巨大的塑像在纽约湾的入口以自由的火炬迎接着世界各地的人们。

2. Complete the Following Dialogues in English with the hints given in Chinese

（1）

A：Good afternoon. Your ticket and passport, please.

B：Here you are.

A：Thank you. Do you have any luggage?

B：Yes. I want to have this bag checked, please.

A：Do you prefer a window seat or an aisle seat?

B：A window seat, please.

A：Here is your luggage tag and boarding pass.

（2）

A：Good morning. Welcome aboard. This way, please.

B：Thank you, Stewardess. Can you direct me to my seat?

A：Certainly, may I see your boarding pass, please?

B：Sure, here it is.

Unit 2

1. Reading and Translation

护　　照

护照是鉴定其持有人作为一国公民的旅行证件。护照还要求别国给护照持有人以安全通过权以及各种合法的帮助与保护。有时在获准进入要去的国家之前，护照还必须有签证（官方签署的证明）。

一般来说，政府签发三种护照：（1）外交护照，发给出国执行政府重要任务的人；（2）公务护照，发给其他政府职员；（3）普通护照，发给因私出国旅行者。

许多国家不要求某些其他国家公民持有护照。例如，马来西亚公民在去新加坡时就不需要持有护照。

签　证

签证是政府官员在护照上签署的证明，以表明该护照有效。旅行者要去的那一国家官员负责为旅行者签证。签证证明旅行者的护照已被检验并得到批准。之后，移民局官员允许持有人进入他们的国家。如官方不许某人进入该国，则可拒绝给此人签证。

2. Complete the Following Dialogues in English with the hints given in Chinese

（1）

A：What's the purpose of your visit?

B：I'm here on business.

A：What's your occupation?

B：I'm traveling as tour leader with a tour group.

A：How long are you going to stay in this country?

B：Two weeks.

A：How many currency have you got?

B：I have 5 000 US dollars in cash.

A：Everything is all right. Hope you'll enjoy you stay in this country.

B：Thank you. I'm sure I will.

（2）

A：Anything to declare?

B：I suppose no, except a bottle of whisky. That's duty-free, isn't it?

A：Yes, one can bring in two bottles duty-free. Will you open your suitcase, please?

B：Certainly. Only personal effects.

A：Is that a new camera?

B：No, it's an old one.

A：May I see it, please?

B：Of course.

Unit 3

1. Reading and Translation

乘飞机旅行

在你最后的目的地，你最好检查一下行李是否有损坏。如果你的行李已经损坏了，你可以马上到航空公司要求赔偿修理费。

这时你要填写一张表格，要具体描述物品的损坏情况。如果航空公司弄丢了你的行李，要向航空公司报失。航空公司会对你的损失负责。

如果你的行李很笨重，你又难于对付，不要着急，因为许多机场都有搬运工，这些人会帮你扛包的，当然是有偿的。

万一你因客满未能乘上预订的班机，而你在停止营运时间之前已在机场登记，航空公司必须赔偿你，除非他们能与另一位旅客商议让给你一个座位。如果你有确认的机票，又按时到达机场，可是因客满你不能乘机，你可以要求机场写一份权利说明书，这张说明书会告诉你如何获得赔偿金。

2. Complete the Following Dialogues in English with the hints given in Chinese

（1）

A：What would you like to drink?

B：What sort of drinks do you have?

A：Orange juice, seven-up, coke and Pepsi, and also mineral water.

B：A coke would be nice. Thank you.

A：Tea or coffee?

B：Coffee, please.

A：With milk?

B：Yes, please.

A：More coffee?

B：No, thanks. But would you bring me a glass of water? I'd like to take some medicine.

A：Certainly, sir. I'll be back in a minute.

（2）

A：Excuse me. Would you mind changing seats with this lady?

B：Not at all.

A：Oh, thank you. That's very kind of you.

B：You're welcome.

（3）

A：Excuse me, what's the actual flying time from here to New York?

B：About 10 hours.

A：Can you tell me what time we'll arrive?

B：Sure. Oh, 7 o'clock in the morning, I mean local time.

Unit 4

1. Reading and Translation

不同的饮食习惯

不同的民族有着不同的烹饪方法、服务内容以及就餐礼仪。例如英国人有下午吃茶点或吃傍晚茶的习惯。傍晚茶包括茶和提神的饼干等。英美人喜欢吃生的蔬菜，喜欢把肉做得半熟。他们一般不吃狗肉。在餐桌礼仪方面，中国人习惯往客人盘子里夹菜，以表示他们热情好客。而外国人对此却不欣赏，认为这样做不卫生。

西方礼仪

（1）把食物剩在盘子里在西方被认为是不礼貌的行为。

（2）当你饿了或渴了时，不要拒绝别人递给你的食物或饮料。

（3）如果需要什么，就直接提出来。

（4）如果你不需要某样饭菜，尽管说：“不要了，谢谢。我不喜欢这个，我想来点……"

使用餐具

与欧洲人进餐时，要右手拿刀，左手拿叉，双手并用，手不离刀叉，直到用餐完毕。他们通常饭后喝咖啡。

与美国人进餐时，你可以只用一只手而把另一只手放在大腿上。例如，你可用右手叉西红柿。需要切肉时，就把叉换到左手，用右手拿起刀来切。然后再放下刀，把叉换到右手来吃切好的肉。要是你突然想起要喝咖啡或橘子汁，那就放下叉再喝。虽然看起来很繁忙，却是为人们所接受的。

2. Complete the Following Dialogues in English with the hints given in Chinese

（1）

A：Did you call for help?

B：Yes. The television is out of order.

A：I'm very sorry, sir. An engineer will come and check it soon.

B：Thank you.

（2）

A：This is the operator. May I help you?

B：Yes. I'd like to be woken up tomorrow morning.

A：At what time?

B：Around 6:30 a. m.

（3）

A：I'd like to have some laundry done.

B：Could you fill in the laundry form first?

A：Where is the laundry form?

B：It's in the drawer of the writing desk.

Unit 5

1. Reading and Translation

地　　铁

地铁在大部分较大的城市都有，如纽约、巴黎、哥本哈根、布宜诺斯艾利斯、悉尼、东京和北京。地铁是地下高速列车系统。世界上第一个地铁系统是在伦敦修建的，自1890年一直运行。地铁比公共汽车运行得更快，效率更高。地铁可以把你送到城市里几乎任何可去的地方。并且，地铁的价钱便宜，又有助于解决城市交通问题。地铁的缺点是它经常拥挤不堪并且噪声很大。

买票时，首先把钱投入一个有狭缝的机器里，然后根据你要行走的路程来选择票价，最后票就会从机器中弹出来。在出入地铁站台时都要用票，所以不要把票扔掉。没有人收票，只有机器。

2. Complete the Following Dialogues in English with the hints given in Chinese

(1)

A：I want to change some money, please.

B：What kind of currency have you got?

A：Pound. What's the rate of exchange for US dollars?

B：Today's rate is ＄1.60 to 1 pound. Do you have your passport with you?

A：Yes. Here it is.

B：Please sign on this exchange memo.

A：All right. Here you are.

(2)

A：Good evening. May I help you?

B：Can I change some Euros into US dollars?

A：Certainly. How much would you like to change?

B：200 Euros. What's today's exchange rate?

A：It's 100 Euro for 142 US dollars.

B：OK.

A：May I have your passport, sir?

B：Here it is.

A：Thank you, sir. Please sign on the memo.

B：OK.

A：Here are your passport and money, 280 Euros in all. Please check it.

B：Thank you very much.

A：You are welcome.

Unit 6

1. Reading and Translation

这是一个身穿匈牙利民族服装的布偶,是游客们最爱买回家的纪念品。布偶身上独特的色彩散发着无穷魅力。但是很少有人了解,它们不仅是纪念品商店里精美的商品,也是有生命的精灵。

这是一种生动的再现,即使在喧嚣的现代生活中也依然存在。

Holloko可能是匈牙利东北部山区最具魅力的村庄,也是世界文化遗产的一部分。

当地人和游客们可以看到旧式的婚礼仪式。新娘要穿行主要的街道,向世人展示她的嫁妆,这象征着家庭的财富。传统还提倡大家都参与进来,这预示着将来子孙满堂。

2. Complete the Following Dialogues in English with the hints given in Chinese

(1)

A：One sparkling water.

B：Thanks very much.

A：Are you ready to order?

B：Yeah, I think I am actually. Could I just have the soup to start, please.

A: That's minestrone, is that all right sir?

B: Yeah, that's fine, and for the main course could I have the chicken please?

A: Chicken.

B: And just some vegetables and some boiled potatoes, please.

A: Boiled potatoes, OK?

B: Thanks very much.

A: OK.

(2)

A: Good evening, sir. What can I get you?

B: A cup of brandy with water and ice.

A: There is your drink, sir. How is your stay here? Everything to your satisfaction?

B: Superb! The view is super and the service is excellent.

A: Glad to hear you say so. Anything else, sir?

B: I'd like something a little stronger?

A: May I suggest a sweet Martini Cocktail?

B: That is wonderful.

A: Here you are.

Unit 7

1. Reading and Translation

世界上最长的河流尼罗河,流经非洲西北部,最终汇入地中海。伟大的人类文明多源于河流两岸,但人类历史上最为绚丽、神秘的是始于尼罗河的古埃及文明。尼罗河谷拥有充足的淡水与阳光,这二者被古埃及人奉为神灵,他们尊称太阳为 Amon,称尼罗河为 Apis。孟菲斯是埃及的第一个首都,公元前 3000 年,它建立为独立王国。而若干世纪以前,尼罗河河水泛滥,冲垮了古都。尽管如此,尼罗河所赋予的远大于它所毁坏的。正如古希腊历史学家希罗多德所言:埃及是尼罗河赐予的礼物。每年洪水过后,土地上都会留下一层淤泥,这是能让庄稼茁壮成长的天然优良肥料。

2. Complete the Following Dialogues in English with the hints given in Chinese

(1)

A: What sort of jewelry do you intend to buy?

B: I should like to look at some necklaces.

A: May I show you gold ones or platinum ones?

B: Platinum ones, please.

A: OK, Miss.

B: What is the price for this one?

A: Five hundred and ninety dollars!

B: That is quite steep. Can you offer a special discount?

A: The price is very moderate.

B: It is rather more than I was thinking of paying.

A: We brought the price down only a few days ago. This is definitely a bargain.

B: OK. I will take it. I want to my initials engraved on it.

A: Oh, that can be done.

(2)

A: Customer: Excuse me. I'd like your opinion about this suit.

B: Salesperson: I'd say the jacket is just right but the pans are too small.

A: Customer: Can you alter them?

B: Salesperson: Sure.

A: Customer: How much is the suit?

B: Salesperson: It's on sale for ￥234.

A: Customer: Oh, I'm afraid I won't be able to afford it. I'd better keep looking.

B: Salesperson: There's no need to rush. We're open till 8:00.

A: Customer: Thank you.

B: Salesperson: If I can be of any help, let me know.

Unit 8

1. Reading and Translation

瓦豪地区因其出产大量的优质葡萄树而著名，这是整个多瑙河流域最富饶、最独特的地区。阳光撒在果园里形成了独特的景致，就像传统画中描绘的天堂。

这个山谷中最好的水果当然是葡萄。采摘后，葡萄经过碾压被制成上等的美酒。在瓦豪山谷的克雷姆斯镇，我们发现了一个葡萄酒窖，你可以在此足足品到140种不同口味的奥地利葡萄酒。

多瑙河水在每个转弯处都会激起人们的遐想，仿佛步入仙境。多瑙河继续着它的旅程，它向东流向一个现代的欧洲，流向一个崭新的世界。

2. Complete the Following Dialogues in English with the hints given in Chinese

(1)

A: The Sun Hotel, please. I have to be there by 6:00.

B: We shouldn't have any trouble if the traffic isn't too heavy. Is this your first trip here?

A: Yes, I've never been here before.

B: You haven't seen the sights yet, have you?

A: No, I'm open to suggestion.

B: Why don't you visit the Statue of Liberty first?

A: That's a good idea.

B: Here we are. That will be seven dollars and seventy cents.

A: Thanks a lot. Here's ten dollars. Keep the change.

(2)

A: Excuse me, but could you tell me if this bus goes to the National History Museum?

B: No, it doesn't. There's no through bus to the National History Museum.

A: I see. Where do I have to change then?

B: You can transfer at 24th street.

A: How far is it?

B: Well, it's only three stops from here.

A: I see. Thanks a lot.

B: You are welcome.

##

1. Reading and Translation

　　语言是文化的重要组成部分。学习一门外语同时也是学习一种新文化。这本应该是充满乐趣的事情，但是在我国传统的英语教学基本是以讲授语法和语言知识为中心的。教师更多地注意语言的正确性，这导致不少学生对学习英语失去了兴趣。尽管他们在英语考试中可以取得不错的成绩，但他们运用语言的能力，特别是听说能力却很难令人满意。

　　为了解决这个问题，英语教学专家与教育部官员已经推行了一系列教学改革措施，其中之一就是允许地方教委在国家教学大纲的指导下选择适合自身的教材。

2. Complete the Following Dialogues in English with the hints given in Chinese

（1）

A: Mr. Black, the itinerary is not proper for the old.

B: Shall everything be slow and relaxing?

A: Yes, they need a relaxing holiday.

B: I will set the morning call at 8:00.

A: That will be too early for them.

B: What about 8:30?

A: Sounds reasonable.

B: Time will be too tight for us if we have to cover regular scenic spots.

A: Don't be upset. They have already given me a list of tourist attractions.

B: OK, Let me take a look.

A: Can you put all the places into our new itinerary?

B: It is a piece of cake.

A: Terrific! They will appreciate it if you can meet their long desires.

B: It's my pleasure. Don't hesitate to get in touch with me, if you run into any problems.

A: Sure.

（2）

A: Excuse me, are you Mr. Johnson?

B: Yes. I am Frank Johnson.

A: I am Tony from Zhejiang CTS.

B: Pleased to meet you, Tony!

A: Pleased to meet you, Frank!

B: Our manager, Mr. Dundas has come to meet you. May I introduce him to you? This is our manager Mr. Dundas. This is Mr. Bush from American Pacific Delight.

C: Nice to meet you, Mr. Bush! Welcome to America.
A: Nice to meet you! It's so kind of you to come to meet us.
C: Oh, it is my pleasure. I hope you have had a nice trip.
A: Thank you.
C: Is this your second time to America, Tony?
A: No, this is the first time.
C: Hope you will have a good time in America.
A: Thank you. I am sure we will.
B: Are all the tourists here?
A: Yes.
B: The coach is waiting in the park. Let's go.

Part IV

Appendix

附录

1. Codes of Major World Airlines 世界各国主要航空公司代码

Codes of Major World Airlines 世界各国主要航空公司代码

代　号		
	国外航空公司	
AF	法国航空公司	Air France
BA	英国航空公司	British Air-ways
CP	加拿大国际航空公司	Canadian Airlines International Ltd.
JL	日本航空公司	Japan Airlines
KA	港龙航空公司	Dragon Air
KE	大韩航空公司	Korean Air
KL	荷兰皇家航空公司	Klm Royal Dutch Airlines
LH	德国汉莎航空公司	Lufthansa German Airlines
MH	马来西亚航空公司	Malaysia Airlines
NH	全日本空输株式会社	All Nippon Airways Co Ltd.
NW	美国西北航空公司	Northwest Airlines Ltd.
OS	奥地利航空公司	Austrian Airlines
OZ	韩亚航空公司	Asiana Airways
QF	澳洲航空公司	Qantas Airways Ltd.
SK	北欧航空公司	SAS（Scandinavian Airlines）
SQ	新加坡航空公司	Singapore Airlines
SR	瑞士航空公司	Swissair
SU	俄罗斯国际航空公司	Aeroflot Russian International
TG	泰国国际航空公司	Thai Air-ways International Ltd.
TH	泰国航空公司	Thai Airways
UA	美国联合航空公司	United Airlines Inc.
	国内航空公司	
CA	中国国际航空公司	Air China
CI	中华航空	China Airlines
CJ	中国北方航空公司	China Northern Airlines
CX	国泰航空	Cathay Pacific Airways
CZ	中国南方航空（集团）公司	China Southern Airlines
FM	上海航空公司	Shanghai Airlines
H4	海南省航空公司	Hainan Airlines
IV	福建航空公司	Fujian Airlines
MF	厦门航空公司有限公司	Xiamen Airlines Co Ltd.
MU	中国东方航空公司	China Eastern Airlines

(续表)

代号	国内航空公司	
SC	山东航空公司	Shandong Airlines
SZ	中国西南航空公司	China Southwest Airlines
WH	中国西北航空公司	China Northwest Airlines

2. Types of Aircrafts 飞机型号

Types of Aircrafts 飞机型号

飞机型号	制造厂商	发动机台数	巡航高度	最大航程	每排座位数	座位个数
A310-300	欧洲空中客车工业公司	2	9 450	6 820	6	204
A310-200		2	9 450			228
A340-200		4	9 450	12 510	8	340
A300-600		2	9 450			274
A320		2	11 920	5 400	6	165
B747-400COM	美国波音飞机制造公司	4			11	360
B747-400		4	10 670	12 780	11	400
B747COM		4	10 670			291
B747SP		4	10 670			291
B747-300		4	10 670		12	660
B707		4			6	155
B767-200		2	11 250		7	214
B767-300		2				225
B757-200		2	10 670	5 890	6	200
B737-200		2			6	128
B737-300		2	10 670	2 923	6	148
B737-500		2			6	133
B777-200A		2	11 000	9 000	10	380
B777-200B		2	11 000		10	292
MD-82	美国麦克唐纳—道格拉斯公司	2	10 060	500	5	145
MD-90		2	10 060		5	153
MD-11		3	9 450	12 500	9	340
BAE146-100	英国宇航公司	4				88
BAE146-300		4				112

（续表）

飞机型号	制造厂商	发动机台数	巡航高度	最大航程	每排座位数	座位个数
YAK-42	俄罗斯柳辛设计集团	3				120
TU-154M		3				164
IL-86		4				350
FOK-100	荷兰福克公司	2				108
YN7	西安飞机制造厂	2				48～52
S34	瑞典					35
MD23	美国					16
ATR	法国					60～72
328	美国					32
DH8	加拿大					52

Glossary
词汇表

a course	一道菜
accommodation train	慢车
accompanying number	偕行人数
account	账户
acidic	酸性的
actual	实际时间
address while in	前往国家的住址
admission/entrance fee	门票费
agaric	木耳
air crew	机组人员
air sick	晕机
airline coach service	航空公司汽车服务处
airport terminal	机场候机楼
aisle seat	靠过道的座位
alarm clock	闹钟
alkaline	碱性的
amber light	黄灯
American Express Card	运通卡
amethyst	紫水晶
ancient pagoda	古塔
antioxidant	抗氧化剂，硬化防止剂
antique shop	古玩店
antique, curio	古玩
antiseptic	杀菌的
apartment hotel	公寓饭店
aperitif	饭前酒
appearance	外貌
appetizer	开胃菜
arch bridge	拱桥
architecture	建筑
aroma	香味
arrival card	入境卡
arrival platform	下客站台

arrival time	到达时间
arrivals	进站（进港、到达）
arriving from	来自……
artery traffic	交通干线
artificial color	人工色素
assistant manager	大堂副理
assorted cold dish	什锦冷盘
assure	保证
at the altitude of	高度
at the speed of	速度
at your request	按照您的要求
athletic equipment	体育用品
automatic traffic signal light	自动红绿灯
Average comfort (3-star)	三星
baby's cot/crib	婴儿床
Bacardi	百家得
back bag	背包
bacon	熏肉
baggage check	行李票
baggage claim area	行李提取区
baggage service	行李服务处
Bailey's	比利酒
baked potato	烘马铃薯
bamboo scrolls	竹帘画
bamboo shoot	笋尖
bank teller	银行职员
bank	银行
bankbook	存折
banquet room	宴会厅
bar chair	酒吧椅
bar	酒吧
barber shop	理发室
barmaid	酒吧女招待
barman	酒吧男招待
bathroom	（客房内的）洗澡间
batik	蜡染画
battery	电池
be in charge of	主管
be missing	不见了
be settled	安排好了

be sold out/out of stock	售空
bean curd	豆腐
beauty parlor/salon	美容室
Beck's	贝克啤
become enlightened	成佛
bed spread	床罩
beef	牛肉
beer mug	啤酒杯
beggar's chicken	叫花鸡
behind schedule	晚点
bellboy/bellman	酒店行李员
berate	严厉指责
berth/bunk	火车铺位
beverage	饮料
bicycles for rent	自行车出租
billiard room	桌球室
black coffee	纯咖啡
black tea	红茶
blanket	毛毯
bleach	漂洗
blocked	此路不通
blouse	女上衣
boarding	登机
boarding gate	登机口
boarding pass (card)	登机牌
airport terminal	机场候机楼
Bodhisattva	菩萨
boil	煮
boiled egg	煮蛋
book	预订
bottle opener	开瓶刀
bowling alley	保龄球场
bracelet	镯子
braised	炖
braised beef	炖牛肉
brandy glass	白兰地杯
breakfast voucher	早餐券
brew	泡茶
brick tea	砖茶
briefcase/portfolio	公事包

bring up the rear	殿后
British pound £	英镑
brocade	织锦
brooch	胸针
brown bread	黑面包
Budweiser	百威啤
buffet	自助餐
bulb	灯泡
bulk tea	散茶
bus/coach service	公共汽车
business center	商务中心
business class	公务舱
butter	奶油
buttered toast	奶油土司
button	纽扣
buying rate	买入汇率，买价
cabin	机舱
caboose	乘务员车
cafeteria	自助餐厅
calligraphy	书法
Calvados	苹果酒
camellia	山茶
camphor	樟树
cancel	取消
captain	领班；机长
car hire	租车处（旅客自己驾车）
card key	卡式钥匙
Carlsberg	嘉士伯啤
carp	草鱼
carriage-way	车行道
carrier	承运人（公司）
carrousel	（行李）传送带
cart	推车
carved lacquer ware	雕漆
cash	现金/付款处
cash desk/cashier's desk	收银处
cashier	收银员，出纳员
causeway	堤
cedar	雪松
central axis	中轴线

ceramic cup	陶瓷杯
chain bracelet	手链
champagne bucket	香槟桶
champagne glass	香槟杯
champagne	香槟酒
change	零钱
charge for overweight luggage	超重费
charter	包机
check in	入住；登机手续办理
check out	结账离店，退房
check sth. out	查某事
check, cheque	支票
checked luggage	托运行李，过磅行李
checking account	支票账户
cheese cake	酪饼
chef	主厨
chef's special	主厨特餐
cherry	樱桃
chicken	鸡肉
chlorella	绿藻
chlorophyll	叶绿素
chopsticks	筷子
chrysanthemum	菊花
cider	苹果酒
circumference	周长
CITS	中国国际旅行社
city tour	城市游
city and state	城市及国家
city where visa was issued	签证签发地
city where you boarded	登机城市
class (fare basis)	座舱等级
clay	黏土
cleanser	去污粉
clerk	办事员
clothes hanger	衣架
cloudy	有云的
clove	丁香
club steak	小牛排
coach pick-up point	大轿车乘车点
coat	女短大衣

coat hanger	挂衣架
cocktail shaker	调酒器
cocktail	鸡尾酒
cocoon	蚕茧
cocoon sorting	选茧
coffee	咖啡
coffee mate	奶精
coffee shop	咖啡厅，咖啡馆
departure to	前往……
cognac	法国白兰地
coin	硬币
Coke/Coca-Cola	可口可乐
cold cream	香脂
cold dish	冷盘
color	色
comb	梳子
commerce (business people)	商业人员
commercial hotel	商务饭店
compact	粉盒
compensate	补偿
compensate for	赔偿
compensation	补偿
complain about	对……投诉
complaint	投诉
conch	海螺
condensed milk	炼乳；炼奶
conducted/guided tour	有导游的旅游
confectionery	糖果糕点
confronted with problem	遇到问题
continental cuisine	欧式西餐
control No.	编号
cooking	烹饪
cope/deal with	处理
corkscrew	酒钻
corn soup	玉米浓汤
coronary heart disease	冠心病
cosmetics	化妆用品
cotton swabs	棉签
counter	柜台，吧台
country of citizenship	国籍

country of origin	原住地
crab meat	蟹肉
cradle	摇篮
cream	奶油
credit card	信用卡
cross road	十字路
crustal movement	地壳运动
crystal	水晶
cubes	块
cucumber	黄瓜
cuff-link	袖扣
cuisine	烹调风格/烹饪
currency exchange receipt	货币兑换收据
currency exchange	货币兑换处
curve road; bend road	弯路
cushion cover	衬垫套
customs declaration	海关申报
customs duty	海关税
customs inspector	海关检查员
customs	海关
cyclists only	自行车通行
damage	损坏
dangerous down grade	下坡危险
date	起飞日期
date of issue	票据签发日期
date of birth (birth date)	出生日期
day	日
sex	性别
decanter	酒壶
deep fried	炸
delayed	延误
delayed flight	延误航班
deliver	运送
deluxe suite	豪华套间
demanding	苛求的
denomination	面额
department store	百货商店
departure	出发
departure card	出境卡
departure time	起飞时间,离开时间

departure lounge	候机室
departures	出站（出港、离开）
deposit	存款
destination country	前往目的地国
destroy	毁坏
detergent	洗衣粉
detoxifying	解毒
diabetes	糖尿病
diamond	钻石
diaper, napkin	尿布
diced	丁
digestion	消化
dim sum	点心
dining car	餐车
dinner	正餐
direct flight	直航班机
dirty/filthy	肮脏的
discomfort	不适
discount	打折扣，折扣
dissolve	分解
distance to destination	到目的地距离
distilled water	蒸馏水
dock	船码头
dome car	旅游观赏车厢
domestic airport	国内机场
domestic departure	国内航班出站
domestic/international flight	国际/国内航班
Dongpo pork	东坡肉
double bed	双人床
double bend road	之字路
double room	双人房
double white lines	双白线
double-sided embroidery	双面绣
down; downstairs	由此下楼
draft	汇票
drain	排水
drawn work	抽纱
dredge up	疏浚
dress	连衣裙
drink	饮料

dry cleaning	干洗
dry goods	服装
dual carriage-way	双程线
dummy, comforter	假奶嘴
duty manager	值班经理
duty-free shop	免税店
ear ring	耳环
eardrop	耳坠
Economy (1-star)	一星
economy class	经济舱
economy passenger	普通舱旅客
egg-shell china	薄胎瓷
electric blender	电动搅拌机
electric clock	电钟
electric razor	电剃刀
elevator/lift	电梯
embroidery	刺绣
emergency exit	紧急出口
emigration control	出境检查
enamel ware	搪瓷器皿
encounter	遭遇到
endorsement/restrictions	(指限定条件)
entertainment department	康乐部
entrance/ way in	入口
escargots	田螺
Euro EUR	欧元
excessive speed	超速
exchange	兑换(钱、支票)
exchange rate	汇率
excursion	远足/游览
exit/way out	出口
exonerate	平反
expectation	期望
expiry date (或 before)	失效日期(或必须在……日之前入境)
express service	快洗服务
express service charge	快件收费
extra charge	额外费用
extra flight	加班机
fabric	布料
fabrics	纺织品

fake	假的
family group	家庭旅行团
family name	姓
farmer	农民
fasten seat belt while seated	坐下后系好安全带
feeding bottle, feeder	奶瓶
female	女
ferment	发酵
fiber	纤维
filament length	丝长
filet steak	菲力牛排
fire exit	火警出口
first class	头等舱
first class passenger	头等舱旅客
First (Given) Name	名
first-aid-kit	急救包
fish	鱼
fixed prices	有定价
flavor	味
flexibility	灵活性
flight No.	航班号
floor attendant	楼层服务员
flower-tea	花茶
FLT No (flight number)	航班号
foggy	有雾的
food and beverage department	餐饮部
for stays of	停留期为……
foreign currency	外币
formality	手续
Foster's	福士啤酒
four heavenly protectors	四大天王
fragrance/aroma	香
free luggage allowance	免费托运行李重量
free of charge	不收费
French cuisine	法国菜
French fires	炸薯条
French roll	小型法式面包
French toast	法国土司
fresh water eel	黄鳝
fried	煎

fried chicken	炸鸡
fried egg	煎蛋
from	起点城市
front desk	前台
front office manager	前台部经理
frustration	恼怒
fully booked	全被订满
garlic	蒜
gate	大门
gate/departure gate	登机口
gauze	纱
genuine	真的
get in touch with	与……取得联系
gin	琴酒
ginger	姜
give me back my territory	还我河山
glassware counter	玻璃器皿部
goblet	高脚杯
Goddess of Mercy	观音
gold jewelries	金饰
good for passage between	旅行经停地点
goods to declare	申报物品
Gordon's	哥顿
government delegation	政府代表团
grade	等级
grape	葡萄
grapefruit	西柚
graph paper	图纸
grease	涂脂于
greasy	油腻的
green light	绿灯
green pepper	青椒
green salad	蔬菜沙拉
green tea	绿茶
greeting arriving	迎宾处
grind	磨
grotto	石窟
ground crew	地勤人员
group visa	团体签证
guide post	路标

Guinness	健力士啤
hair brush	发刷
hair dryer/hair drier	干发机，吹风机
hair lotion	生发水
hair oil/brilliantine	发油
hair pin	发夹
hair-curler	卷发夹
hair-net	发网
ham	火腿
ham and egg	火腿肠
hand luggage/carry-on luggage	手提行李
hand posture/gesture	手印
hand truck	手推车
handbag	女手提包
handkerchief	手帕
handle/settle a complaint	处理投诉
have a break	休息
health center	健身中心，健身房
Health Certificate for International Travelers	国际旅行健康证明书
herbal	中草药的
High comfort (4-star)	四星
historical relics	历史遗迹，历史古迹
hot pot	火锅
hotel	饭店
hotel reservation	订旅馆
hot-water bottle	热水袋
household responsibility system	家庭责任制
housekeeping	客房服务
housekeeping department	房务部，管家部
humidity	湿度
hypertension	高血压
ice bucket	小冰桶
ice maker	制冰机
ice scoop	冰勺
ice shaver	削冰器
ice tongs	冰勺夹
ice-cream cone	甜筒
iced coffee	冰咖啡
IDD telephone	国际直拨电话
imitation	仿制品

immigration	移民局
immigration control	入境检查
immunization	免疫
imperial garden	皇家园林
in case	以防
in the strongest terms	最强烈地
in	人口
incident	事件
indoor swimming pool	室内游泳池
in-flight	飞行中
in-flight magazine	机上杂志
in-flight service	空中服务
information	问讯出
information desk	问讯处
ingredients	烹调原料
instant noodle	泡面
interest	利息
international airport	国际机场
international departure	国际航班出港
international passengers	国际航班旅客
international terminal	国际候机楼
investigate	调查
iron press	熨
irresponsible	不负责任
irritate	激怒
issue at	签发地
issue date（或On）	签发日期
itinerary	行程/活动安排
jacket	外套，短上衣
jacquard	提花织物
jasmine-tea	茉莉花茶
jet aircraft	喷气客机
jewel case	首饰盒
jewelry, jewels	首饰，珠宝
jobless	无业
juice extractor	果汁榨汁机
junket	公费旅游
keep in line/no overhead	不准超越
keep left	靠左
keep right	靠右

key card	钥匙卡
key slot	钥匙槽
key-ring	钥匙圈
king-size / queen-size bed	加大床/大床
knapsack	背包
lace	花边
lacquer ware	漆器
lagoon	泻湖
lake cruise	游湖
landed	已降落
lane auxiliary	辅助车道
lard	猪油
larva	幼虫
late snack	宵夜
laundry bag	洗衣袋
laundry charge	洗衣费
laundry list	洗衣单
laundry service	洗衣服务
laundry soap	洗衣皂
lavatories in rear	盥洗室在后部
lavatory	厕所
lazy Susan	转盘
leek	韭菜
lemon juice	柠檬原汁
lemon	柠檬
lemonade	柠檬水
life jacket	救生衣
life vest under your seat	救生圈在座椅下
light meal	便餐
lighter	打火机
lime stone	石灰岩
liqueur	利口酒,白酒,烧酒
lobby	大堂
lobby bar	大堂吧
lobby manager	大堂副理
local flavor	风味食品
local time at origin	出发地的当地时间
local/national guide	地方/全程陪同
locate	找出
lock	锁

long-life milk	保久奶
loom	提花机
lose	丢失
lotus	荷花
luggage carousel	行李传送带
luggage claim; baggage claim	行李领取处,提取行李
luggage locker	行李暂存箱
luggage tag	行李牌
luggage/baggage	行李
luggage/meal delivery	送行李/餐
luxurious tour	豪华游
Luxury (5-star)	五星
magnifying glass	放大镜
mahjong and chess room	棋牌室
Maitreya Buddha	弥勒佛
make a reservation	预订
make a sightseeing tour	游山玩水
male	男
manager of room division	客房部经理
Mandarin fish	鳜鱼
mark car stop	停车标志
mashed potatoes	马铃薯泥
massage parlor	按摩室
Master Card	万事达卡
measuring jug	量杯
medicated soap	药皂
medicinal	医药的
memorial hall	纪念馆
men's wear	男服
menu	菜单
messy	凌乱的
milestone	里程碑
milk-shake	奶昔
minced	剁碎的
mineral water	矿泉水
minestrone	蔬菜面条汤
mint	薄荷
misplaced	错放,放错地方
misunderstanding	误解
mixing glasses	调酒杯

monastery/temple	寺庙
monastic garden	寺庙园林
money exchange memo	兑换水单
month	月
muffin	松饼
mulberry tree	桑树
multifunction hall	多功能厅
mural	壁画
mushroom with green cabbage	冬菇菜心
nail scissors	指甲剪
nail clipper	指甲夹
nail file	指甲锉
nail varnish, nail polish	指甲油
name of passenger	旅客姓名
narrow road	窄路
nationality	国籍
necklace	项链
needle	针
nightdress	女睡衣
no entry	不准驶入
no through traffic	禁止通行
no turns	不准掉头
non-smoking seat	非吸烟席
noodle	面条
nothing to declare	不需报关
number and street	街道及门牌号
nylon	尼龙
object to	反对
occupation	职业
occupied	（厕所）有人
official use only	官方填写
off-the-peg	成衣
olive	橄榄
on behalf of…	代表……
one way only	单行道
onion soup	洋葱汤
onion	洋葱
oolong tea	乌龙茶
optional tour	选择性旅游
orange juice	橙汁

order	点菜
ornament	装饰品
others	其他
outside air temperature	外面的气温
over	煎两面荷包蛋
overcharge	过高收费
overhead bin, overhead compartment	头顶上方的行李柜
overhead light	顶灯
overweight	超重
ox tail soup	牛尾汤
oxygen mask	氧气罩
package tour/trip	包价旅游
pajama	男睡衣
palace lantern	宫灯
panties	女短裤
pantomime	打手势
parking lot	停车场
passenger conveyer	自动步行梯
passenger plane	客机
passing bay	让车道
passport	护照
Passport No.	护照号
passport control	护照检查处
passport control immigration	护照检查处
pastries	甜点
pavilion	亭子
payee	收款人
payer	付款人
Pay-TV	收费电视
peak flying from afar	飞来峰
peak/off season	旅游旺季/淡季
pearl	珍珠
peep hole	猫眼
pendant	坠子
Pepsi	百事可乐
perambulator	儿童车
perfume spray	香水喷子
perfume	香水
persecute	迫害
personal belonging	随身物品

personal check	个人支票
pH value	pH 值
pickled vegetables	泡菜
pickling	腌制
pillow	枕头
pilot	驾驶员
pineapple	菠萝
place of issue	票据签发地点
plane No.	机号
plane, aircraft	飞机
plaque	匾额
plum	梅花
poached egg	荷包蛋
police box	岗亭
pomade	发膏
porcelain	瓷器
port of entry	入境城市
post office	邮局
potage	法国浓汤
pottery	陶器
pouring measure	量酒器
powder puff	粉扑
precaution	预防
presidential suite	总统套间
press	熨衣服
price tag	标价签
printing and dying	印染
private residential garden	私家园林
process	加工
professionals & technical	专业技术人员
prune	剪除
public phone	公用电话
pupa/chrysalis	蚕蛹
quarantine formalities	检疫手续
quilt cover	被套
rail ticket	出售火车票
rainfall	降雨量
rayon	人造丝
razor blade	刀片
reading lamp	阅读灯

rearing net	蚕网
receipt	收据
reception	接待处
reception supervisor	接待部主管
reception/front desk	前台/总台
receptionist	前台服务员，接待员
recipe	食谱
reclining Buddha	卧佛
red light	红灯
red wine	红葡萄酒
reduce weight	减肥
reeling	缫丝
refrigerator	电冰箱
refund	退钱
registration form	入住登记表
regular flight	定期航班
reject	拒绝
relaxing	休闲的，从容的
remedy	补救，赔偿
remove the excess fat	去油腻
renovate	重修
reputation	信誉
reservation	预约；预订
resident manager	住店经理
resort hotel	旅游胜地饭店
restaurant	餐厅
restore	恢复原貌
resume speed	恢复速度
revolving door	旋转门
rice	米饭
rice wine	黄酒
ring, finger ring	戒指
CNY	（China Yuan）人民币
road junction	道路交叉点
roast	烤
roast Beijing duck	北京烤鸭
roast chicken	烤鸡
roast meat	铁板烤肉
rockery	假山
room maid	打扫客房的女服务员

room rate	房价
room service	客房用餐服务
rough road	不平整路
Rum	朗姆酒
rush products	蒲制品
safe-box	保险箱
safety on board	乘机安全
safety razor	保险剃须刀
safety-pin	别针
Sakyamuni	释迦牟尼
saleswoman	女售货员
sand stone	砂岩
sandalwood fan	檀香扇
sandy	沙质的
sashimi	生鱼片
satellite	卫星楼
satin	绸缎
sauna	桑拿浴室
sauté sliced fish in tomato sauce	茄汁鱼片
saving account	储蓄存款账户
Scanda / Veda	韦驮
scenic spot	风景点
scheduled time (SCHED)	预计时间
scramble eggs	炒蛋
seasoning	调料
seat No.	机座号
second-hand store	旧货店
security check	安全检查
selling rate	卖出汇率，卖价
sericin	丝胶
sericulture	养蚕业
service charge	服务费
service agent	服务人员
set out/start off	出发
settle accounts	结账
Seven-up	七喜汽水
shallot	葱
shampoo	洗发香波，洗发液
shaving brush	剃须刷
shaving cream	剃须膏

shelf	货架
shell carving	贝雕
shirt	男衬衣
shoe shining paper	擦鞋纸
shop assistant, salesman	售货员
shopping centre	商业中心区
show case	玻璃柜台
show window	橱窗
shower	淋浴
shower cap	浴帽
shower curtain	浴帘
shower head	淋浴喷头
shreds	丝
shrimps with Longjing tea leaves	龙井虾仁
shuttle	梭子
sickness bag	机上清洁袋,呕吐袋
sightseeing trip	观光旅游
signature	签名
signet ring	印章戒指
silk	蚕丝
silk fan	绢扇
silk floss	丝绵
silk floss quilt	丝绵被
silk flower	绢花
silk painting	绢画
silk scarf	丝绸围巾
silkworm	蚕
silkworm egg	蚕卵
silkworm moth	蚕蛾
silkworm rearing house	蚕房
silt	淤泥
silver jewelries	银饰
sincere apology	真诚的道歉
single line	单行线
single room	单人间
sirloin steak	沙朗牛排
sit back	休息一下
slices	片
slippery when wet	潮湿路滑
slope	斜坡

slow	慢驶
Smirnoff	皇冠
smoked	熏
smoking set	烟具
smoking seat	吸烟座位
snack	点心
snuff bottle	鼻烟壶
soap flakes	皂片
soap powder	肥皂粉
soap	肥皂
soda water	苏打水
soft drink	软饮料
sold out	卖完了
Some comfort (2-star)	二星
souvenir shop	纪念品商店
special-interest tour	特殊兴趣游
specialty	招牌菜
speed limit	速度限制
speed	速度
spinning	纺纱
spool	线轴
staircase	楼梯
stairs and lifts to departures	由此乘电梯前往登机
stalactite	石钟乳
stalagmite	石笋
stall, stand	售货摊
staple food	主食
stationery	文具
statue	雕像
status	订座情况
steam	蒸
steep hill	陡坡
stele/ stone tablet	石碑
steward	男乘务员
stewardess	女乘务员
stewed with brown sauce	红烧
stir-fried	炒
straw ware	草编
straw	吸管
strawberry	草莓

study/survey group	考察团
stupa	覆钵式塔
sturgeon	鲟鱼
sugar	糖
suitcase	手提箱
suite	套房
sundries	零星小物
sunny side up	煎一面荷包蛋，单面煎
supervisor	主管
supportive and helpful	支持的，有帮助的
suspect	怀疑
sutras pillar	经幢
Sweet and Sour West Lake Fish	西湖醋鱼
sweet osmanthus	桂花树
sweet-sour pork	古老肉
switch back road	之字公路
sycamore tree	法国梧桐
sympathy	同情
synthetic	合成的
take action	采取行动
take the boat	坐船
take the lead	前面带路
tannin	丹宁
tapering glass	圆锥形酒杯
taxi	出租车
taxi pick-up point	出租车乘车点
T-bone steak	T骨牛排
tea	茶
tea basket	茶箩
tea ceremony	茶道
tea dust	茶沫
tea plantation	茶园
tea polyphenols	茶多酚
tea set	茶具
tea tray/board	茶托
teahouse	茶馆
teapot	茶壶
teat, nipple	橡皮奶嘴
television remote control	电视遥控开关
temple complex	寺院

tempting/inviting	令人开胃的
tennis court	网球场
tentative	暂定的
terminal building	候机大厅
terrace	露台
Thai Bahts	泰铢
the Classic of Tea	茶经
the crazy monk	济公
the holy relics of the Buddha	舍利子
theater restaurant	演剧餐厅
theme park	主题游乐公园
think silk	绢
thread	线，丝线
threshold	门槛
ticket	门票
ticket confirm	机票确认
ticket office	购票处
tidal bore	涌潮
time to destination	到目的地时间
time	起飞时间
to cash a check	用支票兑换现钞
to deliver	送
to keep the bill	留发票
to wrap up	包装
today's special	今日特餐
toilet	抽水马桶
toilet articles	盥洗用品
toilet mirror	梳妆镜
toilet paper	卫生纸
toilet soap	香皂
toilet/lavatories/rest room	厕所
men's/gent's/gentlemen's	男厕
toothbrush	牙刷
toothpaste	牙膏
toothpick	牙签
torch, flashlight	手电
tour escort/leader	领队
tour group	旅游团队
tour arrangement	旅行安排
tourism	旅游业

tourist assets	旅游资源
tourist attraction	旅游点
tourist boom	旅游热
tourist ghetto	度假村
tourist resort	旅游胜地
towel	毛巾
tower	楼/阁
traffic light	红绿灯
traffic line marker	划路线机
traffic police	交通警
traffic post	交通岗
traffic regulation	交通规则
transfer passengers	中转旅客
transfer correspondence	中转处
transfers	中转
transit	过境
transit stop	过境停留
travel	旅游/旅行
travel service	旅行社
traveler's check	旅行支票
traveling bag	旅行包
trinket	小饰物
triple room	三人房
trunk	大衣箱
tulips	郁金香
tumbler	平底无脚酒杯
turbulence	乱流
turn left	左转
turn right	右转
twin pupae/double cocoon	双宫茧
twin room	标准双人间，双床间
two-way traffic	双车道
uncaring	不关心的
underpants	男短裤
underwear	内衣裤
unexpected circumstance	出乎意料的情况
unfavorable	令人不快的
unfriendly	不友好
unwilling	不愿意的
up; upstairs	由此上楼

upset	生气
up-turning eaves	翘檐
US $	美元，USD
V. I. P. room	贵宾室
vacancy	空房
vacant	（厕所）无人
vacant room	空的房间
vacationing group	休假团
vaccination certificate	防疫证书
valuables	贵重物品
vanilla ice-cream	香草冰淇淋
vegetable soup	蔬菜汤
veranda	走廊/阳台
visa	签证
Visa Card	维萨卡
visa type	签证种类
vitamin	维生素
Vodka	伏特加
voucher	凭证，券
wall hanging	墙帷
wall lamp	壁灯
wardrobe	衣柜
warp	经线
water jug	水壶
weave	织造
weeping willows	柳树
weever	鲈鱼
weft	纬线
Whisky	威士忌
white coffee	牛奶咖啡
white wine	白葡萄酒
winding road	连续弯路
window seat	靠窗户的座位
wine glass	葡萄酒杯
win-win	双赢
withdraw	取款
women's wear	女服
women's/lady's	女厕
worker	工人
woven rattan articles	藤编

wring	拧，绞
year	年
yellow croaker	黄鱼
yellow wine	黄酒
zebra stripes	斑马线
Zen sect	禅宗
zipper	拉链

References
参考文献

1. 房新海. 旅游英语 [M]. 北京：高等教育出版社，2004.
2. 周玮. 旅行社英语 [M]. 广州：广东旅游出版社，2003.
3. 陆志宝. 导游英语 [M]. 北京：旅游教育出版社，2003.
4. 姚宝荣. 模拟导游教程 [M]. 北京：中国旅游出版社，1999.
5. Benedict Kruse. 旅游业英语 [M]. 北京：外语教学与研究出版社，1997.
6. 杨天庆. 四川英语导游 [M]. 北京：旅游教育出版社，2003.
7. 陈刚. *Greater Hangzhou* [M]. 杭州：浙江摄影出版社，2002.
8. 周刚，牛晓春. 交际英语口语 [M]. 大连：大连理工大学出版社，2002.
9. 常骏跃. 旅游英语口语 [M]. 大连：大连理工大学出版社，1999.
10. 罗伯特·马杰尔. 餐饮英语 [M]. 北京：旅游教育出版社，1999.
11. 陈泰豪. 旅游接待实用英语会话 [M]. 上海：同济大学出版社，1988.
12. 魏国富. 实用旅游英语口语 [M]. 上海：复旦大学出版社，2003.
13. 王爱莉. 实用旅游英语泛读 [M]. 上海：复旦大学出版社，2003.
14. 陈冠蒨. 轻松旅游英语 [M]. 北京：中国旅游出版社，2005.
15. 张秀桂. 英语导游翻译必读 [M]. 北京：中国旅游出版社，2001.
16. 杨斌. 出国旅游应急英语 [M]. 北京：旅游教育出版社，2003.
17. 实松克义. 海外旅行英语 [M]. 北京：外语教学与研究出版社，2002.
18. 常骏跃. 英语流行口语 [M]. 大连：大连理工大学出版社，1999.
19. 袁智敏. 领队英语 [M]. 北京：旅游教育出版社，2010.